CRAFT AND CURRENT

A MANUAL FOR MAGICAL WRITING

JANISSE RAY

T
WILD

CONTENTS

ALSO BY JANISSE RAY

Cover book design by Erin Kirk.

Cover art by Raven Waters, "Ramen Faux Pho," 34 x 54 inches, oil on canvas.

Author photo by Michelle Holloway.

Interior design set in Meridian using Vellum.

Printed in the United Kingdom

First printing, June 2024

Library of Congress Cataloging-in-Publication Data

Ray, Janisse, 1962-

Craft and current / Janisse Ray.

Published by Trackless Wild Books

895 Catherine T. Sanders Road

Reidsville, GA 30453

www.janisseray.com

Inquiries: tracklesswild@gmail.com

For
William Kittredge

MAY I BE THE TINIEST NAIL IN THE HOUSE OF THE UNIVERSE.
MARY OLIVER, *UPSTREAM*

PREFACE

Look, if I can be a writer, you can too.

By all odds I shouldn't have become an author. I was raised a poor kid, but poverty was only one strike against me. I was a girl. I experienced a bunch of shame. I sat at the end of a long line of mental illness.

At seven years old I couldn't imagine what would become of me. I had watched my dad walk through a tall window, attempting to reach some light he believed was god. I had seen sheriff's deputies hie him away in a patrol car, had seen my mother weeping.

I didn't know when my father would return, if ever. I wandered through our four-room house wide-eyed and mute, trying to overlook the worry in my mother's eyes and not ask her questions that scared her. I thought about *The Boxcar Children*, a book my teacher read aloud to my class at school, about four children who lost both parents and lived alone in an abandoned boxcar in the woods. Things ended well for those kids.

Somewhere in the grim months of my father's first nervous breakdown, I learned what could save us.

Stories.

Stories are an unrelenting force. They're stronger than hurricane-force winds, stronger than a river in flood and more rain falling, stronger than a great white shark. I say: Stories can save anybody.

Exactly what would become of me was set in motion during those early years on a junkyard in southern Georgia, with my father orbiting a far and bewildering side of the universe and my mother, tight-lipped, doing what had to be done. That I would become a writer seems unlikely. But it happened. I became a writer of stories aimed at making the world a more empathetic place. My entire body of work—my entire body— began to tilt in that direction.

The world needs stories. Human civilization depends on them. I believe that all stories matter. Your story matters. I for one long to know who you are, what you have seen, and what you know. You matter to life itself. What happens to you matters.

I believe that the highest purpose of story is to reconcile ourselves with what we know to be true, what we believe is true, or what could be true, despite what we are told. Story reconciles us with our mythic and heroic capabilities. It reconciles us to history, to the future, and to the rest of the world. If the arc of time bends toward justice, and I agree that it does, stories push us along.

You have been tapped to tell stories. You want to be a writer. And you'd like to do it well. This book is about writing that transforms—that becomes a divining rod quivering in the hand as it points toward underground springs and rivers.

You know what good writing does to you when you read it —it stirs you deep inside, it moves you. You wonder, *how did that writer do this?* Then you think, *Can I become a writer, one like that? How?*

The question is, *How do you do justice to the stories you've been given?* I can tell you how.

You need three things in order to write killer prose.

1. You need craft. That means you need to learn how to put words together so they say more than what's printed—black symbols on white space—on the page. You have to push your words to say more. And something more than craft is necessary.
2. You need a constant, delicious, and ever-deepening relationship with mystery. How does a writer find that magic? What guides us into the deep sources of our power and shows us how to tap that power and how to transfer it to the page?
3. You need to know how to build this life for yourself.

As I was working on this book, a metaphor kept occurring to me: the craft of writing as a boat, setting out across a pass, a wide expanse of blue water. On the other side of the pass is a golden shore. The writer rows across the pass, from the real and earthly to the mystical and magical, gathers some golden things, and then returns. Back and forth, across a pass, from this world to another—that's how a writer works.

How can you get yourself into that current?

In this book I lay out how to do that. How to write from the ribs out, from the keel up, from the mast down. If you're ready, if you have a destination, if you're on a writing journey, then fit your oars into the locks.

Note

The book is divided into three parts, and in all three I alternate chapters, zigzagging between craft and magic, which you'll see as you begin to ply these waters. Part I is philosophical and substratal. Part II covers tools and techniques, or the more practical aspects of writing. The third part offers resolution, or as I say above, how to build this life for yourself. I've added a few appendices, including a bibliography.

A companion workbook is also available. There you will find the exercises, writing prompts, and general questions, plus space to answer them.

PART I

1

IN THE BAY

I grew up on a junkyard in the south of Georgia. The junkyard was a mile outside a scorching town called Baxley, set in the steamy and fragrant pinewoods of the coastal plains, 70 miles inland from the Atlantic Ocean. The town had about 3,000 residents, mostly white and black, among them a handful of Jewish families and one of Vietnamese refugees. The place was slowly emerging from Jim Crow when I was born, in the process of abolishing "Colored Only" signs, not yet burdened by right-wing dogma.

Baxley, Georgia had a Main Street, a water tower, and a post office with a marble floor where my family's box, number 162, had belonged to my great-grandfather. The town had a juke joint, the Ponderosa, where I never went, and a country club, Pine Forest, where I also never went.

My mother's people were from Baxley, as were my father's people. Both lines shot a long way into the past in that place, and before that, they jumped a series of migrations beginning in the British Isles, with ancestors who were clan-based and tribal, determined and driven to prosper. These folks had emigrated first to New York and Virginia, then progressively moved toward new frontiers as native people were violently pushed out, which is how I came to be born in the southern United States.

In my sleepy, tense, and careful hometown, everybody was connected to everybody else, marginally or profoundly, usually in multiple fashion. Our lives snapped together like Legos. A person without connections was marginal, alien, and dangerous. From these bundles and braids of relationship, stories— the result of the connections made or broken—were born.

Underline that. Stories are the result of connections made and connections broken.

Part of a literature

My father, a junk man, trucked in stories more than he did batteries, alternators, and tie-rod ends. Born into poverty and into a family threaded with mental illness, Franklin Ray was a heroic character, as tall and impossibly handsome as Elvis, complicated like Fred Sanford. He never wore glasses, he never went bald. He was brilliant, larger than life.

People knew my father as a problem-solver (Can this radiator be fixed?) and as a money man (How much will you give me?). When some tension tangled their lives or halted their forward motion, folks visited my father. They arrived at the junkyard to pawn a wedding ring, to sell a set of hubcaps, to make an offer, to pay a visit, to find out. Franklin returned to their houses, riding the straight, hot roads of south Georgia looking for materia to add to his yard.

In this boiler of a town I heard stories endlessly. The characters in the stories were people I knew or people connected to people I knew. The settings of the stories were places I knew. From a very young age I understood myself to be part of a vast, tightly woven, land-based literature, whether I could name it as such or not.

That kind of childhood is, of course, disappearing.

An original tension

My father, however, did not actually want his children to be part of the ever-widening and ever-deepening circles of the world's stories. He knew better than anybody that stories could corrupt, turn us into alcoholics or thieves, make sinners and questioners out of us, plant crazy notions in our heads. God-haunted, Franklin wanted us spiritual and incarnate. Therefore, part of his complicated agenda was to guard his children against the very stories he collected and kept alive.

When my parents married in 1957, like so many families in America they had bought a television, but a year later, when my sister, Kay, was born, my father threw the TV out of the house. Franklin refused to allow his children to be tainted by Hollywood. He also recognized that television was displacing books, and it was displacing the front porch, where stories rose and fell.

Not having a television left me ignorant of pop culture but deeply immersed in literature.

Years later, as a grown woman, when computers were displacing televisions, I took a walk with my father in his tree-grown junkyard. My dad's pants pockets sagged with a revolver he always carried, an asylum of keys, and an Old Timer with a broken blade. He and I came to a Ford coupe manufactured in the fifties. Its tires were long flat, dry and cracked, sunken into swampy ground. The car's curved back glass was thick with a mold or lichen that grew like mini barnacles. My father tapped the glass.

"You see that television in there?"

I scratched off a sphere of lichen to make a porthole the size of a half dollar. "Yep," I said.

"That's the one we took out of the house," he said.

"When Kay was a baby?"

He nodded. "She was young."

"So that's the one," I said. "You think it still works?"

"I don't see why not."

I was reminded of my childhood without television and reminded that instead of television, I was put in hundreds of locations that afforded me the power of stories. Places like my grandmother's porch on a Saturday evening. Mourning doves cooing. Barred owls calling from the branch. Or my mother's kitchen where grease drifted off skillets of frying chicken. Or the marble steps of Baxley's post office. Let me write that sentence again without the list: *In hundreds of locations in my childhood I learned the power of stories.* I was allowed to learn a culture, culture being a set of stories we tell ourselves about life in a place and how to navigate that life.

I believe that a place, in one of its acts of genius, produces artists to tell its stories, and I'm grateful that southern Georgia birthed me.

I thank my parents for the stories. I thank them for forbidding stories. Because of that, I learned to discern.

Public library

My dad, like most of his sisters and brothers, had dropped out of high school. He had enrolled in a business school downtown and earned the equivalent of a GED. He became self-educated and an inveterate reader of encyclopedias, so, although he outlawed television, Franklin sanctioned books. He allowed his children free run of our town's public library.

Back then the public library in my hometown was located between a dry cleaners and the county jail. In fact, the library and the jail shared a parking lot. To enter the library was to walk a kind of gauntlet. Inmates would cat-call us from the barred windows of the jail.

Once inside, we devoured every book in the children's section. I was obsessed by a series of YA biographies of famous people—Annie Oakley, Abraham Lincoln, Pocahontas. I was driven to learn as much as I could about how to live.

Later I was influenced by the work of Marjorie Kinnan Rawlings, author of *The Yearling*. I recognized myself and my geography in characters like the boy Jody and also in Rawlings herself. In her nonfiction book *Cross Creek*, named for the place she lived, 200 miles south in north Florida, Rawlings describes anoles. "They are partial to a warm bed that a human has slept in and expects to sleep in again that night," she wrote.

She called them *chameleons*. Chameleons I knew. We called them *lizards*. From the moment I read that one passage I never looked at lizards the same. Jane Austen or Charlotte Bronte never mentioned anoles. Cross Creek was *my* world, canonized. Reading Rawlings, I became her. I became somebody with worth.

I was not stupid. I knew that people of color, for instance, had a different place in Rawlings's world than white people. Most black people lived in The Quarters, for example, and most white people lived in large houses on tree-lined streets.

Part of the power of story is that we name our world, whether we understand it or not, whether we adhere to its rules or not.

Then and now

A few years ago a package from Florida arrived in my mailbox. In it was a vintage copy of *Cross Creek,* printed in 1942.

"Janisse, I found this book in a thrift shop in Fernandina Beach. As soon as I saw the library it came from, I thought perhaps you may have checked it out as a child. It is a sweet old copy of a wonderful book...enjoy! I work at the Ordway Swisher Biological Station. When I started in 2007, you gave a talk at the Florida Native Plant Conference (you signed my book!) Ten years later and I have grown to know and love this place. If you are ever in the area, it would be my pleasure and honor to show it to you. I have a small farm in Alachua, you are always welcome. Best wishes—Lisa."

The title page of the book is stamped BAXLEY PUBLIC LIBRARY. In the back of the book is a "Date Due" slip. The book was first checked out in 1966, when I was four. That wasn't me. The 11th and final time it was checked out was July 28, 1975. I want to believe that was my hand. I would have been 13.

Censorship

By this time my dad was very religious, a fanatic. As kids our only worry about books was getting them past my dad, into the house, so we could read them. Nor did we dare leave them lying about. My dad might pick up any book and beneath its cover find something to censor—pants-wearing, cursing, running around, drinking. If my dad found sin-talk, he confiscated the book. I saw him burn *Helter Skelter*.

I learned from reading books the duration of my childhood that

- Books open doors.
- Books open eyes.
- Books open minds.
- Books validate lives.
- Books disrupt lives.
- Books are dangerous objects.

Validation

Before long I was slipping through the adult stacks at the library, where I fell in love with Southern writers. They circumstantiated my rich, complicated, and tragic life. I devoured *Gone with the Wind* and *Tobacco Road* and *The Autobiography of Miss Jane Pittman*.

When I finished *Childhood: A Biography of a Place*, life as I knew it ended. Probably I was too young for Harry Crews. My existence had been, at least on the surface, upstanding, domestic, proper, Rockwellian. Crews was gritty, Gothic, tough, irreverent. He had been born in a ratty town 20 miles south, a place called Alma, and reading *Childhood* was as if I sat for a few days on a gray, weather-beaten, rotting porch, listening to cotton pickers and turpentiners and shad fishers, people who subverted the law if the law didn't suit them, who spent time on the chain gang, who cursed and lied, fought and fornicated.

I took particular care to keep Crews hidden from my father.

Then I found *Look Homeward Angel* and *A Lesson before Dying* and *Their Eyes Were Watching God* and *A Good Man is Hard to Find*. In time I would run my hands over familiars on library bookshelves: Alex Haley, Joel Chandler Harris, Walker Percy, William Styron, Eudora Welty. The years passed. Chinua Achebe, Doris Betts, David Bottoms, Ralph Ellison, Shelby Foote, Cormac McCarthy, Alice Walker, Richard Wright.

I started working at my local library the summer I was 14, my first paying job. I learned the Dewey Decimal System before I learned to drive. That seems a pretty good order of things.

How it started

Probably I knew in eighth grade that I wanted to be a writer. That's the year my English teacher, Jerry Carter, assigned 30 days of journaling. I wrote on lined sheets and arranged them in a notebook that I've kept: *Janisse's Jaunty Jocular Journal*. I seriously named it that. The first entry is dated April 22, 1976, a Thursday. I was 14.

"This is my journal. A journal is something like a diary but you can write things like what you did, your feelings, opinions, things you want to remember, and important things. We're writing a journal for my English class."

By Saturday, two days later, I started to get less abstract. "The first thing we did was go unload a trailer full of old crumbly cement blocks. They came from an old house being torn down. The people load the blocks and we have to unload them. The pieces are being used to fill up a low driveway, so it won't wash out."

Then the next Tuesday, "It's true that many people don't realize their advantages or luxuries. They just don't know what it's like to do without something even for a short time. Like hot water. Some people don't even think about it when they run their hot water to take a bath. I do, because I carry it from the stove in a kettle. Okay, I'll explain. About a year and a half ago electricity got sky high. My father tried this experiment about turning off our electric hot water heater for one month to see what kind of change it made. The water heater has been off ever since."

I wrote about a Beta Club trip to Disney World. When I saw vacationers throwing money in wishing wells, I wrote, "I'd guess that if you cleaned out all of those places, you'd get more than $400."

I'm grateful that I received signs early on pointing out my path, in the way an ornithologist friend knew at six years old that he would study birds. For many people this doesn't happen. Sometimes it never happens. Following the release of my first book, after a reading at the Margaret Mitchell House in Atlanta, a short-haired, earnest woman approached me, "I'm 60, and I still don't know what I want to be when I grow up," she said. "I can see you've found your calling. How did you do it?" She gazed at me as if I were a therapist.

"You'll figure it out," I assured her. "There's time."

Yes, she will. You will. Of course you will. There's time.

The purpose of story

Some people believe that art should exist because it is art and for no other reason. The sole purpose of art is to fill the world with art.

I stand on the far side of that philosophy.

I believe art is a catalyst. I believe the medium of books is particularly suited for catalysis.

We are born on to a planet teeming with gazillions of stories. Some of those have taken over and become dominant paradigms, and sometimes the dominant narratives are oppressive. Stories can make us worse people.

And stories can make us better people. I'm all about that sentence. I believe that the purpose of story is to serve the evolution of human consciousness. A story should push along our souls on their bumbling journeys, intent on learning what we are put on earth to learn.

Yes, a story should be art. But I believe that our job as writers—or at least my job as a writer and I hope your job too —is to populate the world with stories of justice and goodwill until oppressive narratives

t

o

p

p

l

e.

You have to find stories that are big medicine and tell them.

Credo

Our job is to populate the world with stories that cause oppressive paradigms to topple. God, what is stopping us? If that is not your belief, please quit reading here. I don't want to show you how to make the world a worse place.

Exercise

If you don't already have a dedicated space in your home that you call your library, walk around and find one. Put this book on it.

Prompt

I believe the purpose of story...

2

DEPTHS

Almost from the beginning of my long love affair with language, I understood that writing well was not only about nouns and verbs, modifiers and antecedents. For stories to matter, they had to operate at the level of strings of words on a page, which was exciting enough, yes, but also at the level of the spirit behind the words.

My life, when I was a child, had a deep and constant relationship with mystery, and not because of anything I did. The mystery was revealed daily through the myth of my parents' Christianity, and it was revealed through a currency of stories that swirled around me, and it was revealed through a people I came from, the old crackers, who were deeply mysterious—immersed in the mysterium, in fact.

Had I studied with a shaman, or a medicine woman, or a *curandera*, my trajectory into the mysterium might make more sense than it does being raised by tinkerers and collectors on a junkyard in the bronzed and leafed bottomlands of southern Georgia.

When I was a child my father told me repeatedly that two

tribes of people "inherit the earth." What that phrase actually meant was "find god" or "inherit god's kingdom." Those two tribes he talked about were the saints and the poets. Christ-haunted, my father pursued a life-mission to be a saint—not a saint like St. Francis or St. Peter, but a normal, everyday kind of saint. That was his dream for his children as well. Being a saint gave you an automatic ticket to eternal life in heaven.

Logically, if poets inherited the earth, poetry, made up of words, was holy text. Being a poet got you to heaven too. The Bible was poetry and my father worshipped it. Before each and every meal we went around the table, each person in my family reciting a Bible verse.

I could *hear* the power in the words.

I'd written a clumsy verse about Thanksgiving when I was eight or nine—"Now what do I spy/ on the table so high/ Is it pudding/ and pumpkin pie?"—and my father had folded the paper carefully and locked it away in his safe. I might, after all, be one of the chosen. That I became a writer in that clicking of tumblers is entirely possible.

I wanted to please my dad more than anything. I could please him *and* walk streets paved with gold. Damn, I wanted that. Maybe that dream of walking golden streets hand in hand with my father is why I tried to become both things, the saint and the poet.

First manic episode

For a brief span during my early childhood my father was "called to preach," and he had started his own church in an empty, concrete-floored building on Barnes Street in Baxley. Apparently his church wasn't built on solid rock, because it didn't last long.

When I was six, my father experienced a nervous break-down, or what later came to be known as a psychotic break. I watched him stand at a many-paned window looking up at a brilliant chimera of sunshine. It appeared to him as a great and consuming source of light, which he believed to be god. Now he was praying to the great light up in the sky. I remember looking out the window, thinking, even as a small child, *No, Daddy, that is not god. That is the sun.*

My father was a tall man with herculean strength. I watched him suddenly crash his body against the window. With its many panes divided by thin wooden grilles, the window could not hold him, and with a terrific splintering of wood and explosion of glass, he rocketed outside. Our house was single-story, and Franklin landed, bruised and bleeding, in one of my mother's flower beds. He would soon be sent off to the state psychiatric hospital at Milledgeville. But not yet, not quite yet.

One night during that mania, he was fiddling with radio dials when he tuned into a recorded sermon delivered by an evangelist from Philadelphia, Bishop S.C. Johnson. He considered himself to be the 13th apostle of god, and his followers called themselves Apostolics, a form of the Holiness religion. My father, crazed and unable to sleep, boarded a train bound for Philadelphia, where he was baptized into a new Apostolic faith.

After that we couldn't celebrate Christmas or Easter or Halloween. Those holidays were pagan. We weren't allowed to date or to compete in sports. Already we couldn't watch television, and now we weren't supposed to read newspapers. We weren't allowed friends, or I should say that we could be friends with kids at school but not outside school. The females in my family—my mother, my sister, and I—couldn't cut our hair. We couldn't wear make-up, jewelry, or pants. Sex outside marriage was certain damnation. We couldn't do anything that struck us from our pedestals.

Two days a week we fasted, not eating or drinking until suppertime.

Some evenings at supper my father might announce, "Tonight is tarrying service." On such evenings he gathered the whole family in the upstairs study to "tarry," meaning to call Jesus's name over and over. We tarried because we hoped that Jesus himself might appear to us, especially our father, who desired his presence the most. When god appeared, he would come as a holy ghost, and he would float around the study, where a set of encyclopedias weighted down the shelves, and he would touch each of us on the shoulder or on the head.

The thing is, I'm sure spirit visited the study, even if I never saw it or felt it.

I've been in an Apostolic Church many Sundays, watching people get filled with this holy ghost and go dancing down the aisles, speaking in tongues. I have prayed to be filled with the Holy Spirit and to be able to speak its indecipherable language.

The tools for being chosen by the holy spirit were given to me in the form of tarrying, fasting, praying, believing. These were early immersions into the mysterium.

ESP

There was more. My father believed in what is called extra-sensory perception. Of course he did. What is god if not an invisible man in the sky, requiring wild, extra-sensory belief?

To this end, Daddy would play a strange game with us. He would pick an integer between 0 and 10, write it on a piece of paper, and ask us to tell him, not by guessing but by *perceiving*, what number was on his paper.

I got pretty good at it. I concentrated on the number, which I couldn't see with my eyes but could sometimes see with my mind. Seeing the number took a while and it took effort. I didn't actually "see" it, of course. The number occurred to me in a different part of my brain than the one that processes visual information. Freakily often the number bubbled up.

"It's a nine," I would say.

"You guess nine?" my dad replied.

"Yes, nine."

"How'd you come to a nine?" My dad liked to withhold information.

I shrugged. "Is nine correct?"

"How'd you get nine?"

"I guess I guessed it."

He would show me his paper then. "Yes, it's a nine. How did you guess that?"

"Nine came to me," I said.

To my father this proved the hand of god. God had communicated the number to me.

Or maybe it proved that my dad himself would inherit the earth.

The horseshoe

Franklin used to tell a story of a person who kept a horseshoe nailed curve-side down above his door. Someone said to him, "You don't really believe that a horseshoe brings you luck, do you?"

"No," the man said. "But it does, whether I believe it or not."

This maxim lay at the core of my childhood: spirit does not need mere humans to give it authenticity and validity. The number bubbled up whether we believed it would or not; the horseshoe brought luck.

Size of the soul

One day when I was older, in a moment of gentle camaraderie, I found myself deep in conversation with my dad on matters of the soul. We were trying to define it. He told me that his opinion differed from the going opinion. "Most people believe that the soul is a small thing that can be found inside the human body," he said. "I don't think so."

"Where is the soul if not in the body?" I said. I'd heard news-of-the-weird about scientists who weighed dying people just *before* death and then weighed them *after* death, and they had surmised that the difference between the two numbers was the exact weight of the soul—the thing that escaped the body when it died.

"It's actually the opposite," my dad was saying now. "I think the soul is a very big thing. The body is just a tiny manifestation of the soul."

What a wonderful thought-experiment that was for me. My body was a steering wheel, driving around this enormous and invisible thing called a soul, and my soul was forever bumping into trees and flowers and other people all over southern Georgia. Heck, it was bumping into clouds.

Nothing looked the same after that.

Doors swing open

One day my father relayed to me a story that I've been unraveling for three decades.

Franklin was a man of parable. Instead of straight, he talked crooked. His nature was to be mysterious, and he tended toward moral lessons.

One day he set out in his Mazda pickup for Savannah, some 100 miles to the east. He hadn't driven 10 miles out Lane's

Bridge Road when rain began, at first mist but soon a freshet. The wiper on the passenger side wasn't working, but he didn't need it. So he kept going.

He was almost to Glennville, 20 miles along, when a tire began to rattle, loud and louder, finally shaking the entire car before he got stopped. He had a flat. Now a deluge had set in. Franklin put a towel over his head, got out, jacked up the car, and changed the tire. Then he wheeled around and drove home.

"I came home," he repeated.

"Why did you turn around?" I asked. That was the question he wanted me to ask, because this was a parable.

"It wasn't the day," he said.

"But you did need to go to Savannah."

He nodded. "Yessir, I needed to go."

"And the wiper on the driver's side was working."

"Yes, my side worked." Part of this game was cat-and-mouse, me teasing out a moral, him being parabolic. My god, he loved crypticism.

"I'm not understanding," I said.

"I received two signs," he finally said, as if talking to a moron. "Two was all I needed."

"The rain and then the tire," I said. "So you turned around because you figured it wasn't the day to go to Savannah."

"You can say that."

I have interpreted many possible meanings from his parable.

- If life throws roadblocks in your path, consider you may be on the wrong path.
- Allow yourself a couple of obstacles before you quit.
- Nothing is worth struggling for.
- Everything has a season, and do it in its season.

Effort versus effortlessness

Why do you think my father turned around at Glennville and drove home in the rain, on a spare tire? Do you think this is a parable of yielding to resistance, or is there something deeply wise in this? Do you, too, wait for signs that you're moving in the right direction? Do setbacks make you reconsider? Do wins make you surge ahead?

I am thinking about this in terms of writing, because writers particularly experience walls and closed doors and shut gates, or, in other words, a lot of setbacks.

My yoga teacher Mary Brown taught me that there is a sweet spot between Effort and Effortlessness. That makes a lot of sense to me. I think my dad was leaning on the side of Effortlessness. Maybe I allow too much Effort.

Path

The larger takeaway, I believe, is that there is a path. In fact, my dad told me that many times. God had a plan for me. Our job is to see it and get to the trailhead. If doors open, we're on the right path. We need to stay at all costs on the path.

Or, to use a craft metaphor, *if* we get to the banks of the river we want to travel down, *if* the boat is watertight, and *if* the skies run blue, we are on our way.

Steeped in this philosophy—whether it was helpful or not and whether I believed it or not—I began to look for my path. The path wasn't obvious, and I looked a long time for it. That I would be given a path but no signage whatsoever, at least none I could read, made no sense.

I looked and looked.

~

Exercise

If you don't already keep a journal, find yourself one.

Prompt

My path...

3

PUSHING OFF

For a while we're lulled by being young. We think we have plenty of time. We can float.

So I kept looking for my path. I got pregnant. My boyfriend and I quickly organized an avant-garde wedding in a field, then delivered a gorgeous baby boy, then made our marriage legal at a Florida courthouse. Within another year we suffered a divorce. I was 27.

Still I looked.

One Sunday afternoon a few years later I found myself hiking a remote mountain road in the Andes. I'd taken my young son to Colombia so I could have an adventure teaching English, but the situation was stressful—dangerous—and I had sent Silas back to the U.S., to my parents, so I could finish the two weeks left on my contract.

I didn't want to teach English in a foreign country. I didn't even believe in obliterating a diversity of languages from the world.

I needed to settle down, onto my path.

I remember vividly my epiphanic moment. A Sunday afternoon, alone, I was hiking an Andean road. I was walking through a bowl of tall, blue-green mountains, the road dusty before and behind. I was missing Silas although I knew we'd be reunited in a fortnight. I passed huts constructed by hand of deep-orange clay, set within small plots of peas and corn. Tropical blooms of impatiens and geraniums spilled from makeshift planters around swept doorways. Children watched me pass. Women appeared to say hello. Subsistence farmers and husbandmen paused hoeing their terraces to pass a few words, *Buenas* and *Cómo está*? Theirs was a beautiful, difficult life.

What was I supposed to do with my own?

I love nature, I thought, and I love writing. Nature and writing. Writing and nature.

Put them together, a voice said.

I missed a step. Nature and writing. Writing about nature. Nature writing.

Why had I taken so long to figure that out? If I'd paid better attention, I would have known: that was my dream all along.

In a fortnight I returned to the United States, retrieved Silas from my folks in Georgia, and returned to Tallahassee, Florida, where I had been living. I knocked on the door of editor Andi Blount's office at *Florida Wildlife* magazine and offered to volunteer. When a job on its staff opened I applied. I joined The Audubon Society. I checked out books on writing.

Two years later I was a single mom working as assistant editor. I had a good job with benefits, a cool kid in a free-school directed by a dear friend, and a two-story rental with wooden floors. At work I wrote chatty articles about fishing rodeos and worm-grunting. I wrote poems late at night and dreamed of writing novels.

I was on the path.

More

There in Tallahassee, working and mothering and dating and dancing, I wanted more. I wanted to write more, write better, write crooked, write square, write penniless, write rich, write whisper, write loud. I wanted to write wilder.

I wanted to be a writer, not a company woman.

Creative nonfiction

One day I heard about a fourth genre. It was called creative nonfiction. It allows a writer to combine fact with personal experience and to use literary techniques to present the material.

That moment, something happened inside me. A spring-head began to gurgle. A mockingbird flew from a cage. A door swung open with a loud whistle.

I'd been looking for this genre, this new thing called creative nonfiction, or rather this old thing newly called creative nonfiction, or CNF, which could be so much like prose poetry and also like fiction. I wanted to write it. I began to study, to read even more, to plan essays.

However, I had a problem. I had no time to write.

Wait, I did have a few hours a month, when my writing group met. The group consisted of four women biologists and naturalists who were also mothers and who wanted to write about the environment and social justice. We gathered on each other's porches to free-write, to alert each other to contests and deadlines, to discuss books, and to talk hesitantly and longingly about our dreams. These women were Susan Cerulean, Ann Morrow, and Mary Tebo.

Flow-writing

I cut my teeth on Natalie Goldberg's book, *Writing down the Bones*, which introduced me to free-writing, a habit of employing abbreviated units of time to generate material. Peter Elbow developed the strategy and wrote about it in his 1973 book *Writing Without Teachers*.

When I was learning to write, I did a ton of free-writing. It is a tool entirely useful for myriad reasons and a practice that has served me beautifully. Free-writing can unstick and unblock a writer. It can produce poetic micro-bursts. It can sink a taproot down into your art or into your heart. It can produce reflection. It's a powerful form of generation.

I don't use it much anymore—instead, I force myself to write scenes as much as possible—but it taught me a tremendous amount when I was getting started. Even now, if I'm stuck about where a piece needs to begin or where it needs to go or what the through-line is, I will free-write. Three- or four-minute exercises often produce jewels in the form of words, phrases, or sentences that I use in finished pieces.

The way it works is to set a timer for five minutes, or 10 minutes, and follow Goldberg's rules, which I'm not listing exactly. You can read her books to learn more.

1. Keep your hand moving.

2. Don't cross out. Don't edit as you write.

3. Don't worry about spelling, punctuation, grammar, margins.

4. Lose control. Try not to think.

5. Go toward the energy.

Professor and author Bruce Ballenger calls it *fastwriting*. Being the nature writer I am, I'm going to call it *flow-writing*.

Meanwhile

My dream was ballooning. It was getting too big for my circumstances. Night and day I could hear it calling my name. Late in
the evening, as Silas slept, I scribbled into a black, hardback
journal my ideas, my feelings, beginnings of poems, and great
first lines. How could I make writing a bigger part of my life?
How could I devote myself to it?

The years stretched before me, and I began to cast about for
a safe way out of confinement.

Could I find a wealthy man to marry? That possibility
seemed remote since I wasn't small, blonde, busty, or wavy. I
was a feminist single mom.

Could I move back in with my parents? The thought caused
my lungs to tighten.

Could I go to graduate school? How could I afford it? That
option scared me.

Could I stay where I was and slowly advance toward my
dream?

One day at work a story crossed my desk. It was an essay
called "Paradise Ranch" that published in the March 21, 1993
issue of *The Los Angeles Times*. The piece was about Gray
Ranch, a 500-square-mile refuge in New Mexico located in an
ecological tapestry called Sky Islands, which are tall mountains
that surround the grasslands of the Chihuahuan Desert.

I checked the byline: Alan Weisman. Ignoring the day's
editing, I immediately crafted a letter to Mr. Weisman and sent
it c/o *LA Times*. "You're doing the kind of writing I want to do," I
said. "How did you get there?" *How did you come to write about
nature and science? Did you go to graduate school? Was it helpful?
Were your studies in ecology or biology or English?*

Kind Alan Weisman answered my letter. Here I need to
apologize for the hundreds of letters I have received from folks
since that moment many years ago, some of which I have been

able to answer and some of which I have not. I thank Alan Weisman. That I still possess his response doesn't say enough about what it meant to me. It set me on a course that I had been tacking toward without a compass.

Weisman wrote that yes, he had a Master's in journalism, which, "taught me nearly nothing about what I actually do."

What he actually did was write freelance stories about environment and culture.

He told me that his total science background was high-school chemistry and a single course in college geology. Regarding graduate school he said, "The one thing valuable about it was a single course in science writing (and I may be talking only about a single assignment within that course), which taught me to listen hard to scientists and ask innumerable embarrassing questions until I could finally translate what they claimed was important to other dunderheads like myself."

One assignment in one class—I took a risk. I began to apply to grad schools.

Your questions

Do you need an MFA to become a writer? No. You do not.

Will an MFA benefit you? Possibly. Very possibly it will set you back. MFA programs churn out thousands of underemployed and unemployed writers, and you could be ground down into the masses.

Can you become a writer on your own? No.

What should you do? You need to study writing, even if you are self-guided, and you do this by

- reading voraciously.
- attending readings.
- speaking with authors and writers.
- taking classes wherever and whenever you can.

- writing every day.
- constantly trying to make the writing better.

What would be an alternative to an MFA? One is a hand-made MFA, a program of study that includes all of the above.

Space

Writing is a calling. It's an impulse that stirs deep within you. A spark starts glowing, and if you listen to it, it will set you on fire.

If *you* wrote *me* the letter that I wrote Alan Weisman, and you asked me how I came to write about nature, how I got there, and if grad school helped me, I would tell you:

What I needed was a space in my life where I could let writing consume me like a conflagration, and I found that in grad school. I was one of the lucky ones. Nobody promised me an easy row up to a candy-filled island, and that was a good thing, because the row has not been easy, and I've never reached an island.

But I have constructed a life of books. I move through the world looking for stories, and when I find a good one, I'm lucky to be able to work with it. I sit and clack two words together, listening to how they sound. Then I add a third. I take some commas and some periods out of my nail apron, and I hammer those in. I listen again and take out some commas.

I do this until the story is told.

Your decision

It's easy—far too easy—to

- roll along with other people's agendas.
- decide to not take your life seriously.

- throw your hands up in defeat or despair or depression.
- stay small.
- opt for ease.
- not do the work.
- let someone else decide how your life is supposed to go.
- allow other people's opinions of you to determine your course.
- get afraid of failure, of what other people think, of ostracism.
- give up.

It's your choice. If you want to be a writer, you get to decide to be one. Or not.

I'm going to love you either way.

Exercise

Give yourself more space to think. Allow yourself time today to sleep and play. Go take a nap. Great ideas come from naps.

Prompt

How can I make writing a bigger part of my life?

4

MYSTERIUM

Learning the art and the craft of good writing is fabulous and necessary. But I have a truth-bomb to launch.

In the end, all craft and all scholarship of the art is only mechanical.

Something beyond craft is needed, and that something comes from the invisible realm.

A strange force

I am not here to change your belief system when it comes to spiritual matters. I myself harbor avant-garde and hard-won beliefs that I have come to on my own, and I would not ask another person to jettison theirs.

However, in writing, spirit should be considered. I have read thousands of pages of writing that fell dead to the ground in front of me. They were not worth reading, not worth remembering, not worth underlining, not worth buying, not worth saving, not worth memorizing.

On the other hand, I have read pages that came alive, that

grew wings that brushed against my cheeks, that clawed themselves deep into my heart, that lit candles inside temples. I have felt myself, deep in a book, transported to some other time and place. I have recognized this transportation as a strange force that some writing has and some writing does not have.

I dare say that most writing does not have it.

I have reached the end of a sentence, or a paragraph, or a page, or a story, or an entire book, and I have looked back, pondering: Where did that goodness come from? This has been especially true with poems—good poems, great poems. Something magical happens.

Maybe, just maybe, this aliveness of the written word can be explained away by craftsmanship. The writer knew exactly what vowel sound to repeat, what verb to use, what image to retrieve.

Maybe.

Then how do you explain the great writers—intellectual, award-winning writers—whose lines are dead to anything except perhaps the intellect, whose pages are withered and frostbitten and diseased?

And how do you explain the writing that pulses like a living thing? Like a heart? Even one torn from the body.

Where it comes from

For many years I engaged in a correspondence with a colleague and friend, the writer Rick Bass. During one period we wrote each other a lot about invisible forces in writing, and one day I received a letter from Rick with words scribbled on the envelope, a reply to something I'd asked him:

> God? Buddha? The only good writing I've ever done never came from me but from someone else pushing my hand across the paper while I sat in the chair. Every time. It came from

somewhere, for sure—and for sure not within. This—egos puff up like little balloons—and the thing, the godhead, drifts on, no longer liking the odor of the place. —

Listen at that: "The only good writing I've ever done never came from me...." God, that takes my breath away. Someone else was pushing Rick's hand across the page.

Psychologist and author James Hillman, when asked to clarify this thing, this god, said,

"It doesn't necessarily have to involve an out-of-body experience during surgery, or the sort of high-level magic that the new age hopes to press on us. It's more a sensitivity, such as a person living in a tribal culture would have: the concept that there are other forces at work. A more reverential way of living."

It comes without us

Often we don't know that we have entered the spirit world. Often we don't know that an invisible force has touched our work.

We can, sometimes, recognize its presence after it has vanished and we have come to our senses. In exhilarating moments we glance back at our work—we read through it—we see something there that we did not consciously create. Interventions come in the form of things like ideas or scenes or titles or words or entire pages appearing out of the blue. We are brought to our knees. Something has been pushing our hand across the page.

Call it a muse. Call it a spirit guide. Call it an angel. Call it god.

Two worlds exist in parallel, the tangible world and the imaginal realm, this world and the other world. Every person has one foot in the "real world" and the other in the realm

- of dreams
- of coincidences
- of gut instinct
- of the feeling sense
- of the subconscious
- of ancestors
- of interventions
- of luck
- of blessings.

Likewise, a good writer has one foot set firmly in the ink of the page and the other in the clouds.

∾

Exercise

This is as good a time as any to set up a wishing space. Call it an altar if you like. A candle would make a great addition to it.

∾

Prompt

Write about a time you felt that something came through you but from somewhere else.

5

STARBOARD

The University of Montana was among the first creative writing programs in the country to offer a nature-writing degree. One joyful day standing on our front stoop on McDaniel Street in Tallahassee, Silas by my side, I learned that I was accepted. I was awarded an assistantship and I'd be teaching English 101 to undergrads.

I started to prepare for an upheaval.

My friend Susan had one contact in Missoula, the writer Glendon Brunk. Glendon was an Alaskan homesteader and a stalwart enviro who had gone to Montana to complete the MFA program. He would publish his memoir *Yearning Wild* (2001) six years before his untimely death in 2007. He offered to let Silas and me land in his guest bedroom.

I turned in my resignation at *Florida Wildlife* and set off cross-country in a dark-green four-cylinder pickup, hauling behind a small trailer packed with our essentials, including a washing machine. I'd partly raised now-six-year-old Silas in a cabin in the north Florida woods, off the grid, sometimes washing clothes in Yon Creek and sometimes driving to a laundromat in town. Whatever I gave up for grad school, I hoped it wouldn't be a washing machine.

Glendon's hospitality was extraordinary, but we needed our own place. Within a week of arriving, I found, serendipitously and providentially, a bungalow on Chestnut Street, one block from the Clark Fork River, which runs through the middle of Missoula. In the case of the verb "found," a Spanish sentence construction would be more apt here—the house *was found to me*. Glendon was friends with the writer Colin Chisholm, also in Montana for grad school. Years later, in 2000, Colin would publish his memoir *Through Yup'ik Eyes: An Adopted Son Explores the Landscape of Family*. Colin lived on Chestnut Street, across from a house being renovated. He had walked over and obtained the name of the owner. When he called me with the info, the rental had not yet been advertised. I snagged it.

The house sported an ancient apple tree in the front yard and a postage-stamp porch. A minuscule living room featured a large picture window, out which we would watch snow fall, collect on the black limbs of the apple, and drift against a white paling fence. I could cross the kitchen in two strides. Silas and I shared the one bedroom.

The house had another small room about the size of a bathroom, an area at the back of a dirt-floored garage. Its sheetrock walls were painted the light peach of sunrise. The room was unfinished but not dangerous, no raw wires dangling. With an electric heater I could write there.

I thought later of Daddy's parable, about being on the right path, watching as doors swing open. So many doors swung open—the door of financial assistance, the door of Glendon, the door of the house on Chestnut.

My father, however, erred in his thoughts on obstacles. Obstacles get thrown up constantly. Any vision involves struggle. You don't stop if it starts raining and you have a flat tire.

You don't ever stop, not until you run out of time.

In the years to come I would at times regret the path I'd taken. I didn't comprehend completely what I signed up for. But then I was giddy with joy, determined, riding an awesome wave.

Kittredge

Grad school started and after convention of my first class I almost could have packed up and high-tailed it home. In one class I got everything I needed.

I'm exaggerating some, of course. Some.

This class was a creative nonfiction workshop with the iconic writer William Kittredge. He was a shuffling, bearlike man who had been raised a cowboy in the ranchlands of the Warner Valley of Oregon. Although he left the ranch behind, he remained devoted all his life to Warner and its stories, as well as to stories of the West writ large.

Here I am reminded of a prosaic line by Albert Camus, in the preface to his republished book of essays, *The Wrong Side and the Right Side*: "A man's life is nothing but this slow trek to rediscover, through the detours of art, those two or three great and simple images in whose presence his heart first opened."

For Kittredge those essential images came from the sagebrush flats of the Western range.

Kittredge was a man who lived and breathed writing, especially nature writing. If story had a body walking around, breathing valley air, bellied up to the Union Hall bar, it was Kittredge. By the time I got to Missoula, in the fall of 1995, Kittredge was in his sixties. That very semester he was starting to transition away from teaching. He'd been at it for 30 years, and it was time to retire. But he wasn't quite ready, so he still taught a class or two a year. I squeezed through a closing door, still—luckily—on my path.

We called him Bill among ourselves and we called him Bill when speaking to him. That's how he wanted it.

Now I call him Kittredge.

Kittredge's companion was the Western nature writer Annick Smith, a brilliant, creative woman exceedingly gorgeous, even glamorous, with shapely legs and white hair that she wore long, down her back. Annick would become pivotal in my life.

Kittredge's workshop met one evening a week. The first night he told our class that we'd each have to write two essays, and we would workshop them, Iowa style. "Workshopping" means that a writer prints everybody in her workshop a copy of her essay, and the following class session the entire class critiques it while she stays quiet, scribbling their suggestions. (The usefulness of this model of workshopping has been stringently questioned. Its success depends entirely on a professor's goodwill, and Kittredge had that in abundance.)

I'd been writing *articles* at the magazine in Florida, but I had not trucked in anything called an *essay*. As with most of us, I'd heard the word "essay" since junior high but didn't know what one was or how to write one, except that it needed an intro, a body, and a conclusion.

Turns out, it didn't.

That semester I took notes in a tiny, 2x3-inch "pocket memo" notebook. The very first line of my notes says, "Have to be careful not to fall into the syndrome that only things that explode are interesting."

Well, my head was about to explode. I was in Montana, far from a Georgia junkyard. I lived a block from the Clark Fork River. I was in graduate school, sitting in a classroom with a bona fide, flesh-and-blood writer.

The next line in my notes says, "We have so many voices—you have to grow up enough to find which one is yours." (Kittredge said this while looking out at 15 fresh-faced students.)

Reading stories as a kid on his ranch in the Warner Valley had changed Kittredge, and he had spent a lifetime poring through books to glean what he could learn from them. Years later, he was still reading a few days before he died. Annick told me this.

From the very first class Kittredge recommended writers to read. I noted Lewis Hyde's *The Gift* and Graham Greene's overseas stories and Annie Dillard's essay on the Book of Luke and James Galvin's *The Meadow*. (See my book recommendations in an appendix of this book.)

Essaying

None of this was telling me exactly how to get an "essay" on paper, and two poor souls, as Kittredge explained, needed to bring in 15 copies of an essay the following week. No way would I be volunteering for that.

"How long should an essay be?" someone asked.

Kittredge looked apologetic or maybe dismayed. He flicked his eyes toward a bank of windows, then back to us students, then to the door. "Fifteen to 18 pages," he finally said. He paused and revised himself. "Ten pages or longer. Over 20 is pushing it." He winced when he said it. I could sense a wavering conviction that we'd amount to anything—that we'd do the hard work, that we'd be obsessed, that we'd one day embody story.

I thought then of Silas. I had dropped him off at a pay-by-the-hour childcare facility until I could find a regular sitter. I hoped Silas was not playing video games. There I was, 32 years old, sitting in class as if I were a co-ed instead of a single mom. Maybe I'd made a mistake.

I knew that wasn't true, however. I was desperate to learn.

The way Kittredge taught, I would come to understand, was with a great deal of what appeared to be uncertainty. He spoke in short clipped sentences, trying, like Faulkner, to say the ineffable, casting off and spiraling wide. His starts and stops came across as shyness and as reluctance, as if he didn't want to be facing young, ignorant, raw writers, trying to hook up battery cables for a jump-start. He said "you know?" a lot, as if perhaps we already *knew* the stuff he was saying, and he could apologize for repeating it and shut up. Or maybe he figured we wouldn't, couldn't, understand what he was saying, and he felt ridiculous even attempting to explain. His "you know?" had a tone of desperation in it.

The general air in the room was confusion. How would a writing student start on something called an essay and get even 10 pages? Obviously Kittredge knew how, since by then he'd published a nonfiction collection, *Owning It All* (1987), and a memoir, *Hole in the Sky* (1992), plus dozens of single essays. He was finishing up the collection *Who Owns the West?* (1996).

Somebody asked how this essay should be done.

"I didn't know how to write an essay either," Kittredge said. "Somebody told me."

Kittredge proceeded then to lay out a schema. I'm going to map it out for you in this book because that formula, if you want to call it that, flat-out and hands-down changed my life. Boom. It was an explosion. I'm not sure I would have become a writer were it not for this detonation, which both blinded me and made me see. This schema was more aptly a treasure chest, which I was not smart enough to unlock on my own, although it was right in front of my eyes, in everything I'd ever read, and it was full of gold. I was then still under the impression that writing was a gift, not an apprenticeship, that it fell outside the bounds of deconstruction because it happened magically.

I actually thought that.

Most everything I've learned about writing to this day is something another writer or editor taught me. Very little I have figured out on my own. Because of that, I'm tremendously indebted to a lot of people.

Bill Kittredge gave me a priceless gift. Not everybody in the room got the gift. I've spoken to a number of my classmates who don't remember the schema at all. We all transform differently. We hear the wisdom that we are ready to receive. That day a muse dipped her pen in my heart. It sounds magical. The strange thing is, All good writing is magical. All good writing happens only through magic. But the magic comes from hard work.

Go figure that one out.

In terms of my own progress, I should have begun sooner to plunder the how-to books. I've learned how to read them now. I have a big filter or maybe it's a sieve at the entrance to my mind. Everything passes through this sieve. What makes sense goes in. What doesn't make sense gets trapped and tossed out. And also this: sometimes the chunks that get sifted out the first time actually make sense months or years later. When I reread books with a new understanding, I feel terrible, as if I should have been more astute the first time. I should have been more mature.

I am convinced that William Kittredge, more than any other professor in this country, has guided students to become published writers. Over the years he taught many students who became successful writers. He taught Andrew Sean Greer, Amanda Eyre Ward, Pete Fromm, Rick Demarinis, Kim Barnes, Judy Blunt, Kim Todd, Colin Chisholm, Jon Jackson, David Gilbert, Glendon Brunk.

So many others.

Me.

When I review notes from his class, I understand why.

In 2017 the Montana Book Festival celebrated Kittredge's oeuvre. Karin Schalm, then creative writing coordinator at the University of Montana, said, "Bill would like to be remembered most for his teaching."

My letter to him

Dear Bill,

If I have never adequately expressed my abiding gratitude, I would like to attempt. I am acutely aware that much of who I have become as a writer is due your guiding influence when I was most eager and ready to learn. I will always believe that forces of spirit landed me in Missoula, under your tutelage, and rocketed me into your spheres of influence. What I learned from you would forever change the narrative arc of my life, a life I have enjoyed and am enjoying; a life where dreams have come true; a life where I have been able to pursue my deepest longings and to watch some of them materialize. I am forever grateful that you read my feeble attempt at a first book and handed it back to me, staggeringly crippled as it was, with hope in your voice. You found something to praise in my ragged first attempt. That made all the difference in the world. My friendship with you and with Annick, who has inspired me in layers upon layers of ways, has been a blessing. I say this with all sincerity.

I have arrived at Hollins University in Roanoke on one of these wonderful writer-in-residence gigs. For the past few years I have had very little opportunity to write, having been presented with some of the roadblocks to creativity that life throws up, including an adopted daughter, aging parents, my father with Alzheimer's, a farm to manage. But I am able again, here at Hollins, to reinvent myself. I arrived two weeks ago with a number of projects to work on. Instead, I found myself two days ago thinking about a book on writing. In the process of searching for material, I found notes from the literary nonfiction workshop I took with you in fall 1995, beginning a week after I arrived in Missoula.

I've done a good deal of teaching over the years, but I've

never been able to approach the material that you brought to our class—affiliation with other writers, a great love of story, working knowledge of the process of writing, a lifetime spent reading. You've been on my mind and I want you to know, again and again, that you made all the difference in my life. Thank you.

J

How I apprenticed

Look, most writers in the 21st century barely study craft. Most don't apprentice the long years needed to attain great writing. Writing that moves people.

I read my way through childhood. I listened to the stories swirling around me. In high school I joined the staffs of the literary magazine and the school newspaper. In college I majored in English, concentrating on creative writing. I began to publish, anywhere I could. I did my first open-mic reading. I helped form a writer's group. I went on to enroll in writing conferences and workshops. I returned to the university for an MFA. I looked for teachers whose work I loved. I wrote them letters. I signed up to study with a great teacher. Then another and another. I read thousands of books.

My life has been a decades-long apprenticeship to writing, motivated by a belief in the power of story to transcend and transform.

If you want to contribute to the clattering and dangerous body of literature, you'll have to reach beyond the boiler-plate and the humdrum. You'll have to *work*, and hard.

I don't take the making of a book lightly. It's not something to rush. It's not something to be flippant about. It's not something to surrender to the ego. I believe in slow books, books that mellow and ripen enough to earn their keep.

First off, a tree has to die to make a book, and trees are

among my favorite things on earth. A book takes an incredible chunk of the earth's flesh—not simply trees but also fossil fuels to move it around, electricity at every turn, and lots of human energy and time. I feel some shame about that, and in those times I think we don't need any new books, no more talking, no more entertainment. We need to get busy planting trees, not making pages from them.

Yet I know the power of stories to transform a person, having myself been transformed by stories repeatedly, and the importance of stories to change society. If a writer is lucky a book will comfort others, thrill them, hold them, inspire them, change them.

Exercise

Write a gratitude letter to one of your teachers. Send it to them, if you can.

Prompt

I first knew I wanted to be a writer...

6

CURRENTS

Even if folks do get an MFA, most miss the magic. Nobody teaches it, at least not many teachers. Most of us have been taught to trust, and trust only, our five major senses. Occupation of a tangible world, therefore, is a reasonable practice.

However, we possess senses beyond the primary ones.

First of all, we have the widely accepted sixth sense of intuition, the gut instinct.

We also have a

- *sense of time*
- *sense of the passing of time*
- *sense of responsibility*
- *sense of being watched*
- *sense of place*
- *sense of self*
- *sense of balance*
- *sense of our body parts*
- *sense of pain*
- *sense of time*

- *sense of beauty*
- *sense of the earth's rotation*
- and dozens more.

All things are not as they appear, places that appear empty may not be, and everywhere is a wild and secret intangibility. I'm here to make a case for the mystery that cannot be explained away—or even that can—and how it may be employed in learning to write and in writing.

So get your horseshoe hung above your writing room door. And do whatever else it takes to find "someone else" pushing your hand across the page.

Luck versus blessings

The minute I use the word "magic," many people automatically think "atheism." I find this strange, since most religions are built on magical thinking. For centuries there has been a movement among religious factions to distinguish organized religion from magic. If I say "I'm lucky," for example, a deeply religious person might say to me, "No, you're blessed." Their point is that all blessings flow from god.

The institution more aptly positioned opposite magic is science. For an intellectual, believing in spirit at the expense of science is a tenuous position.

I discussed this one day with Dan Flores, an environmental historian. I'd taken a class from Dan in Montana and we had become friends. One day we were meandering through a sagebrush flat on Dan's land, where he had shown me stones arranged to line up with the cardinal directions. Now we strolled toward snow-peaked and claret-tinted mountains, behind which the sun set.

"So you believe that truth can only come from science," I said.

"Without a doubt," he said.

"And you don't believe in magic?" I said.

"Paganism fell to Christianity," he said, "and Christ to Darwin. My worldview is that the forces of nature and life can be explained. Scientifically."

"What a poverty to give up myth," I said.

"Look at the reason we have color vision," he replied, stopping. His dark eyes were keen, his mustache brown and thick. "The Hopis believed that boys went off and came back with different colored kernels of corn. That was the gift of color vision. From the gods."

I chuckled. "I love that story."

"What actually happened is that, as a species, we developed color vision in order to see colored fruit hanging among green leaves."

"Okay," I said. "I like that story too."

"I find the scientific explanation infinitely more fascinating than the legend."

"Science is amazing," I said, "but isn't it presumptuous to think that all the universe can be gathered into the confines of the human brain? What about spirit? Visions? Premonitions?"

"Figments of the imagination," Dan said.

"Maybe," I said. "Maybe not."

"You sound like a religious fanatic. All religion is based on this idea of an all-powerful being who is invisible. That's why religion has to talk so much about faith."

"I'm not a believer," I said.

"I think you've given up god in name but not in theory," he said.

I have a few theories, yes, that I haven't given up, and one of them is that without scientific evidence or much evidence at all, I believe in invisibles. Truly, what *about* spirit? What about mystery, ghosts, visions, premonitions, gut instincts, and dreams? What about god?

Springing from place

We humans have a centuries-long, land-centric relationship with the land, and often these intangibles seem more available in connection to place. The more land-based, the more rooted in mystery, it seems.

- From the Kalahari: "Strong ropes connect you with everything in the universe and when it is important to know about the other end of a rope, it will tap or pull on you" and "The ultimate tracking is not achieved with the mind but with the heart."

- From the Western Apache: Sacred stories are tied to places, as Keith Basso details in his book *Wisdom Sits in Places*. Places are actual ancestors, places are watching.

- From the Iroquois: When a person needs a plant, "it stands up where it grows, calling to you. That is why it is easy to find a medicine you seek."

- From the Celts, as Sharon Blackie writes in *If Women Rose Rooted*, "Once upon a time, inside a hill like this, Celtic women were transformed into the wisest creatures in the land."

Was the land a convenient place to situate dreams and visions? Did dreams and visions spring from the land? Did the land allow the space? How does our disconnection from the land rob us? Is the land still a fountain—a source—of these energies? Can a human be more mythic when connected to land?

Exercise

1. Take one step to invite the imaginal realm into your writing life. Place a sacred object or hang a horseshoe, string of prayer flags, photo of a wellspring, or totem in your writing space.

2. Begin to reconnect to your place.

Prompt

I experience magic...

7

CREDO

At this point in my life I have walked in the front doors of hundreds of public libraries. Each one is different. If I'm there as a visiting author, I try to arrive early so I can walk around, feeling the energy of the place.

Libraries used to have a great energy—abundance, ideas, color, brightness, movement—although one person, one sour librarian, can violate that energy and do a tremendous amount of damage. That's never fun. Thank goodness most librarians are generous and kind.

Now libraries are changing, many in decline. I feel a lot of sadness in most of them, but when I find one that's alive I love to walk around looking at books and displays, feeling the energy of just being there. It's like walking through ionized air —waterfall-like, beach-like, thunderstorm-like air.

Some of the best afternoons of my life I have spent in libraries, a bookish hush packed with possibilities. I've sat beside sunny windows, glancing now and then out into the world, the books like pastries, like delicacies, and also like towering barricades. Libraries have been, to me, prospect and fortress and refuge. I don't know how I would have managed without books.

Change

For thousands of years, changes in society happened glacially. Humans lived for millennia in relationship with the earth, learning how to better survive on it, and in relationship with their groups, learning how to make them work. With the advent of industry, change *itself* sped up, until the world in 1900 was almost unrecognizable to a person born in 1800. The world of 2000 was inexplicable to a person born in 1900. The world I live in now is in many ways unrecognizable from the one in which I was born, in 1962.

We are living in a massive upheaval of culture (a cancel culture of its own). From seed-saving to corporate hybrid seed, or from a mule to a self-driving Tesla—cultural reorganization is happening fast.

The next new thing is here and gone. Two months after the movie release we won't even hear the word "Barbie."

With the rise of television and then computers (both of them more or less during my lifetime) I have watched books become less relevant in the cultural landscape.

This could be a palatable turn of events were I not deep into a lifelong love affair with books—as a reader, a collector, and a writer. It also would be more palatable were not so many other things I love disappearing.

The contrarian philosopher and hospice reformer Stephen Jenkinson wrote about the decline of books in *Come of Age: The Case for Elderhood in a Time of Trouble.* Jenkinson's nonconformist roots, like mine, are wedged in the counter-culture movement of the 60s, which for all its flaws produced stunning thinking and lasting cultural change.

In *Come of Age*, Jenkinson recounts walking the aisles of an airport bookstore before a long flight, looking for a book but finding nothing that interests him.

> Really, they're not even bookstores. They are grottoes of grim fascination with technology, and they are selling gizmos that promise to enhance the reading experience but are clearly helping to make books—the paper kind, what they call now the bricks-and-mortar of the trade—a nostalgic memory. This is something that is happening in your lifetime.

The gist is that books are becoming a nostalgic memory. I see this, and I know you see it.

Look at the bestseller lists—how many books had to sell to get you on the list in 1980 (a million) and how many have to sell now (12,000, I heard most recently).

Look at libraries—their focus on computer access.

Look at the library parking lot in my town—empty.

Look at the average number of minutes an American reads per day—20 minutes for most people, closer to 45 for people over 70.

Change is upon us writers, books becoming nostalgic memories. But listen, if you're a writer you can't focus on *decline*. You have to focus on the *power* of books—a power that story, however presented, will always wield.

Anne Trubek, then head of Belt Publishing, in her Substack called "Notes from a Small Press" argues that the past was not so much the democratic, book-loving time as we want to think of it. She talked about how writers in the past got published.

Here's her list:

- *Most came from wealth and/or had elite education.*
- *Many had a social world of influential friends.*
- *Few could be said to have succeeded mainly on "hustle" or "merit."*

- *(Only one, I think—Toni Morrison—was a mother.)*

In another bit of positive thinking, she says, "There are far, far, far more options for authors to have their books published today than there were at any time in the past. Self-publishing has made gatekeepers an option rather than a necessity, and offers writers the freedom so many desire. There are far, far, far more small presses, university presses, and non-Big Five presses for authors seeking a different experience than the Big Five."

Options are one thing, but the decline of books is real, and what can we do about it?

- We can keep reading, some every day.
- We can take our children to the library.
- We can read to kids, as parents or as volunteers.
- We can read to each other.
- We can visit the library ourselves.
- We can construct and stock a Little Free Library.
- We can attend readings.
- We can maintain a personal library.
- We can write the best books and stories possible, ones that make a reader loathe to put them down.

Power

The fact remains—the pen is a dangerous instrument. A story can be TNT. This is why oppressive governments kill writers. It's why the Nazis gassed journalists. It's why I wanted to write this book.

Stories help us:

1. Deeply connect with each other.

Through the portals of literature we learn about the possibilities of life. We see how others survive what happens to them. We get into the minds and hearts of others.

2. Become more humane.

When Milkweed Editions brought out my first book, an environmental memoir titled *Ecology of a Cracker Childhood*, printed in its pages was their credo at the time: "We publish with the intention of making a humane impact on society, in the belief that literature is a transformative art uniquely able to convey the essential experiences of the human heart and spirit."

I believe this too.

3. Counteract lies.

My teacher William Kittredge had an unusual theory about literature. In the mid-1990s he postulated to my class that creative nonfiction was gaining popularity—so much so that CNF was absorbing fiction—because of capitalism, of all things.

Corporations need to sell us things, so they have to advertise. They say, *If you buy this, you'll be popular. You'll smell good. You'll get dates. Boys will like you. Girls will like you. You'll like yourself.* But advertising became mostly a bunch of lies. Therefore, corporate culture was systemic dishonesty.

Corporations took on the job of telling us their stories and those stories became our dominant narratives—*new iPhone, second home, Sugar Daddy, latest model, bigger lips, nicer clothes, fancier car.* In a confusion created by a noisy, disconnected industrial life, we lose track of our own stories and identities, wants and needs. This causes all of us to absorb stories with our radar flipped on. We are forced to choose constantly what stories make sense and what do not.

Therefore, we read creative nonfiction for its truth. We read it to avoid being lied to, to avoid being oppressed. We seek to reconcile ourselves with what we know to be true and to distance ourselves from falsehoods.

4. Find each other.

Besides needing a cadre of consumers, capitalism needs a workforce, so it asks people to give up homelands, neighborhoods, families, clans, and landscapes, to travel wherever we're needed for work. We leave the familiar, familial, and beloved for educations, internships, jobs, careers. We leave our hometowns and our homes. We never go back. Because of this, philosopher and author Kathleen Dean Moore surmised, in a now-classic interview with Derrick Jensen in *The Sun* Magazine March 2001, that "we lead lives not of quiet desperation but of relentless separation."

Creative nonfiction is one antidote to a vast and growing isolation wrought by separation. CNF invites us into the homes and minds and landscapes of others, places increasingly hard to enter. We read it to find out if another human has learned something that will help us live more meaningful and happy lives. We read it to be together. We read it to hear other people's stories, since the front porches and post office steps are disappearing.

We are people starving for story.

5. Change outcomes.

I believe that most of us constantly seek to transform into better editions of ourselves. We want the world to transform into a better version of itself. Because of this I believe in the power of literature to change one life or the entire world.

~

Exercise

Write your credo, a paragraph about what you believe about writing, books, and story.

~

Prompt

Why I write...

8

MUNDIS IMAGINALIS

The advent of science, which paralleled the destruction of myth, began in earnest with Plato, Socrates, and Aristotle. Then French philosopher Rene Descartes, 1596-1650, pioneered a revolution by developing a scientific method with four precepts.

1. Doubt everything.
2. Break every problem into smaller parts.
3. Solve the simplest problems first, then move toward more complicated ones.
4. Be thorough.

In this worldview any problem or mystery can be solved. Therefore, what followed in the wake of Cartesian thought was an eagerness to believe in human mastery over every other form of life. We humans were better than everything else. We were smarter than trees, smarter than wolves, smarter than polar bears, smarter than St. John's wort, smarter than pink quartz. That position set up a hegemonic duality between humans and nature, with humans having dominion.

Dominion is control.

With this intellectual positioning civilization began to go wildly astray. The human mind is not dominant over nature, nor is it the apex of life. In fact, the limitations of the human mind are made clear to me on an hourly basis. Every cancer patient I encounter makes clear these limitations. So does every schizophrenia patient. So does the destruction of nature. Also the atmosphere.

For Descartes, nature was a *res extensa*, a bare and inhospitable, even demonic, field. It was devoid of soul. In Cartesian thought the soul was tiny. In fact, Descartes located it in the pineal gland, which is about the size of a dry chickpea and can be found in the very middle of the brain.

In the centuries that followed, science reigned over all forms of knowing and being, pushing farther and wider against the mysteries of the universe, attempting to explain everything and minimize the inexplicable, or what Deepak Chopra calls "nonlocal realms." The model of science became an uphill line. The farther we explored, the more we uncovered. The more we believed in our own dominance. We probed the bottom of the ocean and the far reaches of the universe. We studied the depths of the cell, the nature of viruses, the newly discovered subspecies.

More than science

Joseph Campbell, American scholar of myth and archetype, wanted people to understand the power of symbol in our lives. He blamed our flight from nonlocal realms on more than science. He believed that *three* things had transformed human life so deeply that, in his words, in a science-driven world the "long-inherited, timeless universe of symbols collapsed."

One cause, yes, was the development of the scientific method.

Second was "the democratic ideal of the self-determining individual," which meant the end of community.

Third was the invention of the engine-driven machine, which separated humans from the earth.

There were more. "Nor can the great world religions, as at present understood, help us," Campbell wrote. "For they have become associated with the *causes* of the factions, as instruments of propaganda and self-congratulation." He called Sunday morning "a religious pantomime." The rest of the week it's business ethics and patriotism, he said.

"Dead are all the gods," Nietzche wrote in *Thus Spake Zarathustra.*

What happened to our primal way of being in the world? To Campbell's list I will add more reasons for the dying-out of non-rational ways of knowing. Secularism and monotheism, and also empiricism, colonialism, and capitalism. That's a lot of isms, I know. I would add, too, what we call technology, by which I mean the computer.

Here's a list for you.

- science
- the ideal of self-determination
- the machine
- monotheism
- secularism
- empiricism
- colonialism
- patriotism
- business (capitalism)
- the computer

Duality

This set up a long-lasting and virulent duality between science and mystery, with one thing standing in opposition to the other. The truth is either this or it's that. It's not both. It's black or white, not gray. The word "versus" came into favor. James Hillman called duality a "comfortable habit in the Western mind," as in science versus mystery.

visible | invisible
seen | unseen
conscious | unconscious
mechanical | mythic
reductive | expansive
linear | spiraling
linear | circling
linear | braiding
mortal | immortal
analytic | analogic
earth | multiverse
earth | heaven
real world | *mundis imaginalis*
real world | otherworld
real world | underworld
life | afterlife
logic | old astrology
matter | mind
practical | transcendent
particles | myths
reason | metaphysics
natural | supernatural
mechanical | instinctive

Humans are a future-imagining, language-pushing, tool-using, emotion-driven species that prod and press the limits of knowledge. We wrap ourselves in facts. We cheer when we shrink the boundaries of ignorance. We love the theory that never fails us.

We have wandered horribly far—you can see how far every minute of the day—from a functional relationship with places, with our place-based languages, and with the myths of our places. We're long divorced.

Where to find spirit

For writers to be science-based is easy. It is easy to explain away The Weird as coincidence or as figments of the imagination, as Flores suggested.

Sometimes, however, if we are lucky we find a place where all science is worthless, a place where we see a world misty and shadowy and inexplicable and vast and layered.

And something speaks to us.

In our brains, we know, there is a scale. In one bowl of it we pile pieces of spirit we have uncovered. In the other bowl we pile our reasoning. As I wrote in *Wild Spectacle*:

> Here is the crux of the matter. We know magic to be true; we know magic to be a lie. So a line gets drawn inside us, and we proceed to try to find this line: How far do we abandon Spirit, how much do we trust Science? How far afield do we go in search of magic? Somewhere between the two we humans totter.

I'm science-positive, and yet I believe that humans are spiritual beings moored by spirit and connected to each other and to all living things by it. We are attached, all of us, every cell in our bodies, to everything in the universe. The strings that tie us together are lines of spirit.

~

Exercise

How do you define magic? Where, if any place, do you find it?

~

Prompt

I don't know...

9

BURDENS AND LOAD

On my father's junkyard just outside the town limits I was raised to be godly and quiet, good and good-looking. I was a Southern girl in a subset of unedu-cated, dirty-fingernailed, whip-you-if-you-don't-sit-there-and-act-right, working-class people. Yet, my father studied Moses, who led the Israelites out of slavery. My dad had suffered poverty as a child, and he identified with victims.

As a young girl I was presented with the particular tension

- of both accepting and challenging.
- of both enduring and acting.
- of both behaving and not behaving.
- of feeling both shame and power.
- of both resignation and deliverance.

My father whipped me if I talked back.

He whipped me if I didn't speak up. Once he whipped me for allowing a neighbor boy to stomp a turtle to death.

All this is to say that I felt the threat of violence if I intervened or if I didn't intervene. I suppose it was not duality, but it was confusing.

Cultural revolution

Once I was grown, I was lucky enough to fall in the sphere of unequivocal people who worked for world change. These were words they used, *world change*. They were people who belonged to peace coalitions, banked at credit unions, marched for civil rights, emerged from closets, quit shaving their legs, drummed in full moon circles, practiced holistic medicine, enrolled their children in alternative schools, refused to pay war taxes. These people wanted to end racism, classism, ageism, sexism against women, sexism against men, homophobia. Their motto was *Reimagine everything.*

Now we call these people "hippies." "New-Agers." "Potheads." "Granolas." We call them names so we don't have to take them seriously. We call them "boomers," derogatorily, as in "Okay boomer."

Whatever.

An astounding amount of transformation happened in the decades of the 60s and 70s. Those were heady, exciting times. I'm glad I lived through some of that. You can make your times heady and exciting too.

Oppression

When I was a young woman, at the exact time I was learning to write, I began a study of oppression. As I labored to find my voice as a writer, I struggled to find my voice as a human living in the twentieth century in the United States of America, a country founded philosophically on the ideals of freedom and democratic rights, but built ironically and tragically on subjugation and extermination of entire groups of living beings.

Because I was born one I want to look out for underdogs. By "underdogs" I mean beings who have no voice, especially wild species. Beings whose voices are less audible, including children, people of color, single parents, migrant workers, Native Americans, draftees, innocent civilians in times of war, and immigrants. The unsuspecting and unarmed and unabled.

Transformation

The basic movement of life is transformation. The carbon cycle is a transformative process, I once heard religion professor Mary Evelyn Tucker say. Trees breathe in carbon and breathe out oxygen.

The water cycle is a transformative process. So is the phosphorus cycle. And photosynthesis. Weather is transformative.

Buzzards are transformative, David Bottoms pointed out in his wonderful poem, "Under the Vulture-Tree." They have "mercy enough to consume us all and give us wings."

Our bodies are not static, degrading like granite, but are responsive, resilient, and ever-changing. The natural tendency of our bodies is toward function, which is why wounds scab and blood clots and broken bones knit and cells replace themselves. They heal, and the process of healing is transformation. Rebuilding.

Coming from darkness, from nothingness, we humans pursue light and somethingness. I believe that we desire to transcend.

At least I do, and you do.

I desire to transform into a wilder, more coherent, more functional person. I desire to transform the world into a wilder, more coherent, more functional habitat. With this desire burning, I study transformation.

Sure, we are sometimes misguided, and instead of transforming, we stagnate, give up, and destroy, and then our effort or lack of effort culminates in disaster.

Sometimes, too, instead of transforming into better versions of ourselves, we change for the worse. The very avenues for positive transformation can be used for bad. For example, psychologist Dr. Yukio Ishizuka says that a close interdependent relationship is more critical to fundamental change than a therapist. Yet, the same close interdependent relationship can destroy a person—consider adverse childhood experiences, for example.

How people change

I want to give you a list of ways that people transform, both for the better and for the worse.

- Intimate relationships, especially the warm love of at least one person in childhood
- Experience in general
- Therapy
- Drugs and medications (especially psychedelics)
- The sun
- Diet
- Religion
- Listening
- Institutions—the university, the military
- Trauma
- Adverse childhood experiences
- Nature
- Death
- Stories

How do stories transform a person?

As a child I listened to my father telling stories of transformation from the Bible, about a man raised from the dead or how a few fish fed multitudes. Also I heard my father read aloud verses like Psalms 119:130, "The unfolding of your words gives light, it gives understanding to the simple."

So stories are the transformation I know. When stories transform me, I am heartened by their power. When my stories transform others, I am over the moon.

Empathy

Story allows a reader or a listener to escape the confines of our own built environments and enter the world of another. Stories utilize our biological ability to empathize. They invite us to imagine another's plight or understand a larger idea.

Stories of the "other" are the scaffolding of empathy. Immersion in story when I was most impressionable drove home what my father already demanded of his children before a supernova sucked him away, that we understand the art of empathy.

In my father's paradigm, empathy required action. For example, a heron struck on the highway required that my father splint its broken wing. An elderly man who knocked at my dad's door on Christmas Day meant taking his tools in pawn. Also gathering up a box of food.

A good story leads to action.

Silence

Silence is asked of us on so many fronts. We are silenced by family values, by the economic class we occupy or want to occupy, by our education, by our ethnicity, by our gender. Fear silences. Loyalty silences. Love silences. Most of us are taught very well to be silent, to live in cultures of censorship, so much so that we easily internalize fear and silence ourselves.

Oppression flourishes in silence, which is why Martin Luther King, Jr. said, "Our lives begin to end the day we become silent about things that matter."

Self-censure

Never do I teach a writing workshop without writers grappling with silence. They worry about what their family will think, what their town will think, what friends will think, if they write what they know. Will someone be hurt? Will someone be angry? Will someone go to jail?

One of the more common ways writers silence themselves is with insidious rhetoric they speak to themselves. It goes like this: *My story is not important. My story is boring. My story is embarrassing.*

"Writing is a struggle against silence," said Mexican writer Carlos Fuentes.

Courage

As there is a connection between oppression and silence, there is one between people of courage and writers of books. On March 6, 2002 an article appeared in *The New York Times*, "India Jails Novelist for Criticizing a Court Ruling."

> The prize-winning Indian novelist Arundhati Roy was sentenced today to a day in jail and a $42 fine. The Supreme Court convicted her of criminal contempt for having suggested that the court was trying to "silence criticism" of its approval of a hydroelectric project.

Stories start movements, document movements, end movements.

Validation

Our civilization is not furthered so much by the Kardashians and Hiltons of the world but by *all of us* adding sticks as fuel to this fire we're building, which is our *culture*. We don't find meaning by watching a few "stars," but by studying constellations formed by many voices, many characters, and many epiphanies, yours included. Story validates your identity. Story gives you a sense of agency, of personal power. Story validates all of us.

Your story is important.

Your story is full of complexity. It's definitely not boring if you write it well.

You may have figured out something that I need desperately to know. I'm interested in you.

My telling you that your story is important, of course, is not enough. You have to tell yourself those transforming lines. You have to learn to believe them, and if you can't believe them, to move past your outer and inner censors and do the work anyway.

Lying

Transformation is difficult when sources—media, the church, the status quo, the ruling class, criminals—tell us a different version of a story than what is true. Lies are destructive because they warp our knowledge of reality. They are a form of oppression. They block transformation.

Adrienne Rich writes beautifully about lying and being lied to in her essay "Women and Honor: Some Notes on Lying," which published in the seismic text *On Lies, Secrets, and Silence*.

"I allow my universe to change in minute, significant ways, on the basis of things you have said to me, of my trust in you."

"To discover that one has been lied to in a personal relationship, however, leads one to feel a little crazy."

"The unconscious wants truth."

"An honorable human relationship—that is, one in which two people have the right to use the world "love"—is a process, delicate, violent, often terrifying to both persons involved, a process of refining the truths they can tell each other."

"Lying is done with words and also with silence."
"When a person tells the truth she creates the possibility of more truth around her."

Your truth

To get to a place of scary truth I often guide writing students through flow-writes beginning with, "What I would say if I told the truth" or "What I'm not supposed to say." Writing starts to get interesting when the censors hush.

Once I heard the writer Dorothy Allison deliver a lecture at Berry College in Georgia. Born in South Carolina, she wrote about her childhood traumas, including sexual abuse, in a powerful and moving book that published as fiction, *Bastard Out of Carolina*.

"Writing true stories is in resistance to lies."

"I write against ignorance, against stereotype."

"Honor the truth that builds healthy souls."

Untruths

Sometimes we lie to ourselves, punishing ourselves with word-bombs. *I am not good enough. I can't. I don't know how. I don't have enough money. I'm not pretty enough. I'm not white. I'm not a man. I'm not a woman. I'm not straight. I can't walk. My parents never went to college.*

We lie to ourselves when we block out stories that challenge our world-views, or frames. We sometimes use our privileges to warp our stories. We use the ways we lack privilege to warp our stories.

Remember

The basic movement in life is transformation. We humans, I am convinced, desire to transform into better versions of ourselves. Story is one great avenue, out of many, for transformation. Story leads to transformation because of our ability to empathize. Censure and self-censure can silence us, so it's important to tell ourselves the truth about who we are and what amazements we can accomplish.

∾

Exercise

What privilege do you enjoy?

∾

Prompt

The truth is...

10

SUPERSTITIONS

Maybe you're not trying to be a mystic, you just want spirit appearing to assist you as you work.

A few years ago I was introduced to the book *Ensouling Language* by the late Stephen Harrod Buhner. Buhner was an animist, an herbalist, and a healer. Over the course of his career he wrote many books about a land-based or animist existence, including *Plant Intelligence and the Imaginal Realm* and *Sacred and Healing Herbal Beers*. Many of his works are how-tos, philosophical gems hidden beneath such titles as *Herbal Antivirals* and *Herbal Antibiotics*.

I already had tremendous respect for him because his herbal protocol for overcoming Lyme disease (*Healing Lyme*) saved me when six months of IV antibiotic therapy couldn't, and as he says, one looks at plants differently when a plant saves them.

Buhner began *Ensouling Language*, his how-to writing guide by trashing Strunk and White's *The Elements of Style*. That's because Buhner approached the craft of writing from the opposite direction. What writers are looking for, he said, is the ability to re-create the experience of reading a text that transforms us. We are reading a story—we get a feeling of *wow, holy smokes, something just happened to me—the front of my shirt is wet with tears and I didn't even realize I was crying. Wow.* We wonder how the writer did that. Understanding how to move a reader is what an apprentice writer needs to know, not style.

Buhner says, "For those of us who are meant to be writers, this is a mythic journey and a mythic profession. We learn how to intentionally dream and by dreaming enter mythic realms in order to write what we write...we must learn to let the mythic flow through us and onto the page."

I read *Ensouling Language* to the last page. Then I did something uncharacteristic, even unthinkable. I turned back to page one and began the book anew. This was the first book I ever read like this. I had not understood fully Buhner's theories, and in many ways I still don't. But that's the place I want to rattle toward.

The feeling sense

Buhner's wonderful book is well worth buying and reading. I'm going to summarize his fabulous idea about how to make your writing come alive. Buhner was convinced that to get to a place where magic happens in your writing, where the mysterium swirls about you, is via a particular feeling sense. "The element that is crucial is your capacity for empathy, your capacity to feel," he wrote.

I feel. People feel. We all feel. We are a feeling species. It is this ability that matters most in writing—the ability to feel everything, to feel as deeply as possible, to feel what is not being said, to feel what cannot be seen—and to name that as your truth.

But the word "feel" has to be defined because there are

many ways of perception. Buhner lists three and I have added a fourth:

- kinesthetic—bodily—*I feel my face burning from the sun.* Or, *I touched the kettle. It's hot. I feel my heart racing.*

- emotional—interior state—*I feel confused. I feel happy. I feel giddy.*

- energetic—the invisible made physical, similar to kinesthetic feeling but different—*I feel a buzzing in my hands.* If you do energy work, such as polarity therapy or reiki, you can feel energy. It moves in circuits through your arms and torso with a buzzing, river-running kind of feeling. Sometimes it makes your stomach growl. This is what poet Rachel Guido deVries meant when she told me she hovered her hands above a book to feel its power. (This is the feeling I added.)

- environmental—atmospheric—exterior state—This is how a location, object, or situation feels to you. *I feel as if something is about to happen. This restaurant doesn't feel right. This is the perfect seat for me. I was meant to be here. Oooh, that person feels threatening. This one feels good. I feel a weirdness between the two of them.* (Sometimes the only word we have for this feeling is "weird." The feeling will land in our bodies —a chill or a thrill passes through our chest or a tiny alarm at the base of our skull buzzes or sometimes a general feeling of easiness or uneasiness overtakes us.)

Ask the question

Buhner says, "Of everything ask, How does it feel?"
  How does this chair feel?
  How does this cup feel?
  How does this hotel feel?
  How does this rehab center feel?
  How does this medicine feel?
  How does this therapist feel?
  How does this book feel?

How does it feel?

Great writing depends on the way a person feels their environment, or this thing Buhner calls "nonphysical touch." Here's
how nonphysical touch works: You see. You feel what you see.
You ask yourself, *How does it feel?* You describe it in words.
Buhner called this "a reclamation of ourselves, an ecological
restoration of our interior world and a restoration of our
capacity to feel."

  If you can't see, you simply *feel*, palpably and impalpably.

  We're trained away from the mysterium. We're not taught
ways to access it, to reach into it, to pay attention to it. This
happens daily with the reductionism of science and religion
away from mystery, until we get more comfortable with linearity, and vice versa, uncomfortable with nonlinearity. We don't
want to be the brunt of jokes, so we join the scientists in chuck-
ling at mystery.

  We have a fear of wildness, a fear of the ability to transcend
humanness.

  We get convinced that the feeling sense does not exist.

  However, we are not the only species with intelligence, with
communication, with tool-making, with meaning-making, with
the understanding of the other. Every living system has a

neural network, often larger than our own. Look at the mycelial networks of entire forests, how fungi on the roots of trees act as conduits for hauling resources throughout a forest. This kind of new science undermines the entire reductive worldview.

A caveat

In an early writing class in the 1980s, when I was a coed at Florida State, a woman professor introduced me to the idea of qualifiers. Women are more likely than men, my professor told me, to use words like "maybe," "probably," and "likely." They are more apt to talk about feelings or at least say "I feel," as opposed to men, who are more likely to say "I think." The prof's lesson stayed with me.

Therefore, I have tried to speak with more certainty and to rely more heavily on the intellect in the same way that I attempt to train myself away from saying "I'm sorry" too much, apologizing for problems that are beyond my control or that do not require an apology.

However, I now know that rejecting a feeling sense may be one more way women have been asked to give up the imaginal realm. What is wrong with a bit of healthy uncertainty? What's bad about feeling? Remember, we can remove qualifiers from our writing without burying our intuition.

Library of feeling

This brings us to words. English is woefully inadequate in its feeling words.

Let's look at the word "adore."

I adore this cowboy hat.
I adore my dog.
I adore my children.

You don't love your new Frye boots the same way you love your baby. We all understand this and work with it. But it's good to name as a limitation that the single word "love" is asked to perform a wide range of functions in our language, and thus the meaning of the word is confused and diffused and mitigated.

"What we cannot speak about, we pass over in silence," said the Austrian philosopher Ludwig Wittgenstein.

This means that you are going to have to expand your vocabulary of feeling words—alive, happy, joyful, depressed, tense, sad, enraged, hurt, peaceful—so that you become exquisitely literate about what you feel. We have to build a library of words that will allow us to adequately, beautifully and richly describe what we see and feel.

≈

Exercise

Think about how the place you live feels.

≈

Prompt

My place feels...

11

SUNRISE

Transformation in story happens in a moment of change called epiphany, a glorious flash of recognition all writers seek because it's what makes literature so powerful. Kittredge said that epiphanies can be thought of as "moments of insight or flashes of understanding in which we see through to coherencies in the world." He said, "We are all continually seeking such experiences. It's the most commonplace thing human beings do after breathing." He called it the primary and incessant business of our lives.

Stories, then, have the power to change everything. Through stories we can create a world in which more of us are able to experience our lives as transformed and transformative.

When impact is gradual

Instead of in a blinding flash of comprehension, change also happens quietly, over time, like wind-erosion. Juan Ramon Jimenez's lovely little poem, "Oceans," is about this kind of transformation.

I have a feeling that my boat
    has struck, down there in the depths,
    against a great thing.
    And nothing
    happens! Nothing....Silence......Waves.....

—Nothing happens? Or has everything happened,
    and are we standing now, quietly, in the new life?

Is all art transformative?

"In some sense I could argue that all art is a form of activism," Egyptian-born poet and professor Matthew Shenoda said in an online interview with Negesti Kaudo, in the ezine *Mosaic: Literary Arts of the Diaspora.* "All art is in some manner an intervention in a larger conversation about society and humanity and a present moment." Stories start conversations and continue conversations.

However, as Shenoda pointed out, art can uphold the "dominant narratives of a given society" and serve as a kind of "ornamentation" or "anchor" for oppression or destruction. We have many dominant and destructive narratives: That police are not at fault for wanton killing of our young black men. That white is superior. That men are stronger. That queer is immoral.

On the other hand, Shenoda said, art can "trouble those narratives" by questioning the world around us. As the Nigerian novelist Chimamanda Ngozi Adichie said, "Stories have been used to dispossess and to malign, but stories have also been used to empower and to humanize. Stories can break the dignity of the people, but stories can also repair that dignity."

Peter Forbes, who left a corporate environmental job to co-found the Center for Whole Communities, an eco-justice retreat center in Vermont, wrote a piece called "The Circle of Story, Vision, and Leadership." It examines the power of story to change the world, and in it Forbes said that story "can be the resistance of our heart against business as usual."

M.K. Asante, Zimbabwe-born author of the memoir *Buck*, calls this kind of writing "artivism." The genre includes Thoreau's great essay, "Civil Disobedience," Pablo Neruda's poetry, Alice Walker's fiction.

As Kittredge wrote in *Taking Care*, "Useful stories, I think, are radical in that they help us see freshly. That's what stories are for, to help us see, and reinvent ourselves." And he said, "We need stories that will drive us to care for one another, all the creatures, stories that will drive us to take action. We need stories that will tell us what kind of action to take."

Artivism

In 2003 I was invited by author and activist Tony Dunbar to submit an essay to a collection by Southerners who were defenders of the poor, believers in racial equality and the rights of nature, and opponents of militarized American society and untethered capitalism. That book became *Where We Stand: Voices of Southern Dissent* (2004). It was followed by *American Crisis, Southern Solutions* (2008), which questioned many forms of fundamentalism.

Much of my work hopefully will be classified as activism, because I am consumed by a need to live more sustainably on our planet so that we don't destroy ourselves and everything we love. Every single paragraph I've written is a call to action and an attempt to shine a spotlight on a better path forward.

Greatness

In high school one of my English teachers, David Raby, assigned me a question: What is true greatness and what does it mean to you? I struggled with that question because I was not reared to think about greatness. I was reared to think about getting a job, getting by, making a living, having faith in god, and ignoring nature because nature was dirt, backdrop, lumber, venison. This question opened me to the idea that greatness can mean different things, and that I too might wish for greatness and attempt to reach it.

Power

There are two kinds of power. One is hierarchical, power over, *public power*, which can lead to sad and even horrific conclusions.

The other is *personal power*, which believes in individual potential, that of yourself and all others. Personal power is the ability to make your own life go well without infringing on the ability of others to make their lives go well.

Leadership, then, is not a role or a position to hold on to, but an activity that frees other people to find their personal power.

Source

One source of my personal power is language, inherited from my father, with his Anglo-Saxon roots and his Elizabethan Bible—figs and grape leaves, psalms and commandments. In childhood I committed Bible verses and poems to memory. I listened to the cadence of old-timers speaking their dialects and terminologies, Gullah and Hebrew and Celtic.

The source of my power is words, the depth and range and strength of words.

The source of my power is my hand, a hand with a pen, the pen moving, the words building.

This is a power not to be taken lightly. Worlds can be created with words, with language, and with the spirit bonds linking words; and worlds can be destroyed. Said another way, we can build a wall with words, and the wall can protect a garden or it can shut someone out. Writers have to be careful.

Voice

I'm thinking of the gift of voice, of the body's voice but also the larger voice of words printed on cellulose, shooting from presses, pages of words. Words coming from the mouths of woodpeckers, strings of words woven into the nests of birds, howling words, words wrapped around the trunks and limbs of trees. Your words. My words.

I'm thinking of what we can do with this power, how we can lever it to more transformation.

I'm thinking how it already has brought me so much, the chance to meet and interact with and love so many people. It gives me gifts I would as a child never dreamed.

It can do the same for you.

The world is painfully beautiful, the world is a map. We are travelers, all of us, and our most important narrative is the one of our lives, which includes the learning, the great epiphanies, and the unwinding. The most important voice is our own.

Mandate

If your life too has been transformed by literature, and if you too can be counted among the people who believe in the power of story to transform, and if you want to lend your voice to a better world, then your task is to learn how to transform ideas into compelling, imaginative, useful stories.

You as hero

When you're writing personal narrative of any kind, you become the de facto protagonist of your story. This thing happened to *you*. You survived it. You overcame it.

You're the hero. You did do something heroic, something worth celebrating. You went on a hero's journey and you made it home.

(I use the word "hero" here in a non-gendered way.)

Now you're writing about it.

When you get past all the viper-pits of shame and the judo-holds of imposter syndrome and the miasmas of despair, your work takes shape. Alas, you begin to think of yourself as a hero.

You find a publisher and then the heroism gets exceptionally potent, because the job of the publisher is to push the fact that you are a hero, so that your books will sell.

I want to tell you something. *You are not the hero of your work.*

Who is the hero?

Your reader is the hero.

Your reader is the one who is showing up, looking for glittering jewels that will change their fortunes, and also looking for treasures to carry back to their people. The reader does the hard work of opening their mind and reading. The reader is the person who transforms.

Not you.

You already did.

Levitate a room

Once I was in residence at the lovely Vermont Studio Center. One evening a well-known poet came to speak. I happened to sit in a row next to a witchy writer—I got her outspoken, potion-stirring vibe right away.

After the reading, as we left the theater side by side, the witchy writer said to me. "He is not a poet."

"Pardon?" I asked. A full orange moon perched on a clock-tower that loomed over the town.

"Those poems were all *me* poems, as in 'Look at me,'" she said. "Those were not *we* poems. Poetry is about *we*. A poet should levitate a room."

Years later I remember her words almost exactly.

"Me" culture

Social media cultivates a "me" culture: *look at me, watch me, listen to me, pay me.*

New York publishing creates a "me" industry: *look at this new superstar* or *look at this old superstar.*

Whoever's work is selling is the hero, and a popular way to make sales is hype. If enough money gets thrown at promotion, people will not notice if a book, for all practical purposes, is unreadable. I've seen that happen hundreds of times. Don't get me started listing the best-selling, award-winning, and unread-able books.

I'm saying this loud and clear. I want you to remember where you heard it. Remember that Janisse told you.

You may be a hero, but you are nothing without a reader.

The reader has to see themself in your work. They have to see themself as your main character.

You are an alchemist and a spell-binder. But not a hero.

Artists are transcendent

One of my heroes is Howard Zinn, late professor of political science at Boston University, where he taught Alice Walker, and author of the truth-telling *A People's History of the United States.* In an essay that became a small book, *Artists in Times of War,* Zinn wrote,

> By transcendent, I mean that the artist transcends the immediate. Transcends the here and now. Transcends the madness of the world. Transcends terrorism and war.

How do we as artists transcend?

We can recognize that our work transcends the "I." We can ground local or personal stories within the larger context of a common story. We can offer a reflection or a vision. We can let our hearts open to the other.

Then our job as writer becomes one of reading our own hearts and turning those meditations into story, remembering always how lucky we are we get to do this powerful work.

Consider your job, then

Stories are powerful. They transform. They are medicine, they are shrooms, they are lovers, they are vultures.

May they consume you and give you wings.

Exercise

Think about these questions: When do you lie? When are you silent? What are you most afraid of as a writer? What is your power? What is true greatness to you?

Prompt

The source of my personal power is...

PART II

12

STORY

We bandy the word "story" about as if everybody understands what we're talking about.

Story is a thing we create, a thing we write, a thing we want to get out in the world. But what is a story? What must a story have in order to be called one?

I ask my students, in university classes and weekend workshops, to tell me their definition. After a long silence someone will say, "Something that happened?"

"Great answer. What else?"

Somebody else will say, "Something that didn't happen?"

"Yes! Keep going."

From dozens of brainstorms I've collected multiple dozens of answers, all interesting and correct, assuring us that the word "story" avoids linearity and reduction.

What is a story?

Something that happened
Something that didn't happen

A series of events
Something worth passing on
A legacy
A created world
A teaching vessel
A rewriting of history
A specificity that points toward a generality
A revelation
A way of seeing
A perspective
Emotional appeal
Universality
Opportunity
A lesson that's taught
Relationships
Conflict
A journey
Retelling of life
A recollecting
A reckoning
Opening and closing
A portal—a provocation
Ordering or shaping of chaos
Escape
Map of how to live
A harvest
How culture transmits itself
A controlling idea
Insight
The why of a person's ideas and feelings
A narrative—something happens
A sequence of action
Different kinds of truth
Parable, allegory, myth

Container for emotion
An offering
An experience
A personal interpretation of reality
Hope and epiphany
A message to readers—an author's intention
A connection to a reader
A connection to a common human experience
An understanding
An attempt to understand, meaning-making
A gift of feeling
Framed piece of knowing
A collection
Contemplation
Resolution
Conflict—tension—details
Explanation
Make-believe, perception
Sharing—instructing—entertaining—teaching
How we remember our ancestors
The brain turned inside out
A taxidermy, preserving memory
A healing
An ordering or shaping of chaos
The construction of a mythology

Beginning, middle, and end

Usually in a brainstorm someone will arrive at an English Department definition of story, "a narrative with a controlling idea that contains a beginning, a middle, and an end."

That works too.

A great definition

Peter Forbes, in his essay "The Circle of Story, Vision, and Leadership," defines story as "the narrative of what has happened to us, shared in a manner that conveys what we believe in relative to those experiences." He goes on to say that story is also the process of listening to and witnessing someone else's experiences.

Why stories move us

In 2009 a fan sent me a copy of an article that appeared in *The Charlotte Observer*, "In search of Tolstoy readers – in a Twitter world" by Joel Achenbach of *The Washington Post*. Achenbach was interested in why people still read long-form narrative when it competes against "incrementalized information," meaning minimalist forms such as mobile phone novels, Twitter posts, micro-essays, or charticles (combinations of text and graphics.)

Story isn't just cultural, Achenbach said, it's biological. "Narrative isn't merely a technique for communicating." Story is how we organize information, how we make sense of the world.

As babies and toddlers our brains cocoon us in immediate needs and wants. Around age four, however, we develop something called "theory of mind," when we begin to understand that other people have feelings and thoughts, the same as we. Therefore, we can feel the emotions and imagine the thoughts of others. We can get inside another's head. We can empathize.

And we do.

It's a giant leap, from our own little world into another's, and this leap allows for, even begs, stories. We want to understand what happened to the other, to Anne Frank, Huckleberry Finn, George Washington Carver, Harriet Tubman, Laura

Ingalls Wilder, Abraham Lincoln, Varina Davis, Kurt Vonnegut, or the Lorax. What we learn from others informs our own lives, our own world.

Because story is biological, Achenbach believes, it will never go away. Even in the age of technology, "the storytellers know that the story is the original killer app." The story, not the gadgetry, is what's irrepressible. "Bloggers aren't storytellers," he wrote. "They are partisans, ranters, linkers. Bloggers give away their entire plot in the first sentence."

Metaphors

Novelist Gary Smith called story "the pipeline to the heart."

One of the most beautiful metaphors comes from Wendell Berry. Stories are leaves. They fall all around, disintegrate, and turn into humus on the ground, which becomes earth. Take these stories, Berry advised, "and turn them into account." Berry said that a human community must "build soil, and build that memory of itself—in love and story and song—that will be its culture." Leaves build humus, stories build culture.

We are stories

In his book *Taking Care: Thoughts on Storytelling and Belief*, Kittredge compared stories to maps that tell us how to get where we want to go. Stories "help us see, and reinvent ourselves."

Then he said that stories are more than maps. They are our selves.

> What we are is stories. We do things because of what is called character, and our character is formed by the stories we learn to live in...Without storytelling it's hard to recognize ultimate reasons why one action is more essential than another.

We lie in bed, waiting on sleep, and we work up the narratives of our lives—who we will marry, what home we will buy, how we'll raise our children, what we'll do with a tax refund.
Our best story is the story of our own life.

So

If every human is a character in an important story, and

- if stories are maps,
- if they are pipelines to our hearts,
- if they are the leaves that build the soil of our culture,
- if they are medicine, boats, rivers, spider webs, and mycelium,
- if they are permanently a part of human evolution,
- if they are transformative and the route into empathy,

then the job of the writer starts looking very important. Writers begin to look like change-makers, like cultural creatives, like thought leaders, like holy people.
Do you see what I'm doing here?
I'm letting you know that yours is a big job. Your writing is life-giving, even sacred.
Devote time to it and get good at it.
Since you are the main character in your story, write a great one.

Obama

In his 2008 presidential campaign, candidate Barack Obama knew that he had to establish a narrative about his life or another would get established for him.

The politician Obama understood the power of story, potent and unforgettable. He understood the power of connection, and he determined that personal story was the most essential and also the quickest way to connect.

I signed up to volunteer for his campaign and was trained by a south Georgia firebrand named Jeana Brown. Jeana was a white woman native to the coalfields of West Virginia. She was married to an African-American long-haul trucker.

She said that, according to national protocol, there would be no training without a chance for volunteers to tell their own stories. She went first. "When I first saw Obama speak on television," she said, "I thought, *this is my life.*"

Then Jeana asked for stories from the volunteers in the room.

Nathan was a progressive in a deeply conservative state. His ethics were to lift everybody out of poverty, as he had been lifted.

Raven was a handsome political junkie with an intense drive to make the world better. He was also my husband.

Jimmy was a heavyset, fire-and-brimstone preacher. He had been a racist, he said, and he had preached racism from the pulpit. Then he had a dream. In that dream Bobby Kennedy was approaching him and calling his name, "Jimmy," calling to *him*, the preacher. When Kennedy reached him, Kennedy said to Jimmy, in the dream, "You're not doing right." Months later, that dream left Jimmy's voice trembling. The preacher experienced an epiphany because of a dream in which Bobby Kennedy asked him to do better, be a better person, and treat others better. Now here he was at an Obama training, signing up to register voters.

What my life is like

In the documentary "Running With Our Eyes Closed," Jason Isbell says that writing is like us saying, "Will you listen to what my life is like? And let's compare."

Will you listen to what my life is like? And let's compare.

I like that. I don't think it gets to the massive power of stories, but it's a start.

If you're struggling with why people would want to read you as a writer, then think about what I just said to you—stories help us empathize, stories change the world, stories matter. Also ponder Jason's words—stories let us know what your life is like, so we can compare ours to it.

Now

I hope you don't waste time with self-doubt. Just get the first word down.

Exercise

Ignore everything I just said about story and write your own definition in a dozen words or less.

Prompt

My story starts...

13

LIKE AN INSECT

Creative nonfiction has three basic parts, and these parts snap together in various ways, expected and unexpected, to create structure.

The holy trinity are scene, reflection, and summary. All elements of craft—things like description, setting, character development, lyricism, and so forth—operate within these elements. I'm no fan of deconstruction, but the inability to identify the elements of prose will seriously hamper your ability to write.

Scene

is the showing. A scene in a unit of time in which movement, often in the form of an interaction, happens. This movement can be real motion, a body in action. It can be inner movement. It can be verbal. It can be imagined, which is still a body in action.

The movement says, This happened, then this happened.

Scene is important because the human mind, and in this case the mind of the reader, functions best when presented with movement, as opposed to motionlessness, and with the tangible and sensual. A writer needs to show people walking around wearing things, doing things, saying things, eating things, smelling things, and dreaming things. Stuff needs to happen. Scene invites the reader into the narrative.

The best essay I've ever read on showing is Flannery O'Connor's classic piece in *Mystery and Manners* called "Writing Short Stories." Everything she says about fiction in that essay applies to creative nonfiction. She says, "No reader who doesn't actually experience, who isn't made to feel, the story is going to believe anything the fiction writer tells him" and "Fiction writing is very seldom a matter of saying things; it is a matter of showing things."

Many people who think they want to write have difficulty identifying a scene or recognizing the difference between showing and telling, because the difference is both subtle and glaringly apparent. Like riding a bike, once you can recognize a scene, you always can.

Here is a scene lifted from my journal:

Our class met one afternoon on the top floor of the library, in the university archives. An archivist, a pale woman wearing silver glasses, had shown us Civil War diaries, slave schedules, historic correspondence, and ancient manuscripts. When class ended, my student Ash lingered, waiting for the other students to leave.

She stood very close to my elbow. Her dark hair was bleached blonde starting two inches from the roots.

"I don't want to be here," she said, as if she and I had been talking all morning.

"I'm sorry?" I said. I meant that I couldn't understand what she was saying, for her to start again, please. I thought I smelled alcohol on her breath.

"I don't want to be here. That's why I'm on academic probation."

"You mean you don't want to be in school?"

"Right."

I glanced at the archivist, who seemed intent on putting away the old books she had arranged for us on a wooden table.

"That's why you've been absent? Haven't turned in your papers?" The first paper Ash submitted to me had outlined her multiple attempts at suicide. And I did smell alcohol.

"Yes," she said. "I don't want to be in school."

"Are you the one paying for your education?" I asked.

Ash's eyes were gray. They darted, two foxes in a cage. "Yes."

"You have to borrow money to pay for it?"

"Yes."

"So you're telling me that you're going into debt to flunk out of school," I said. I glanced toward the main floor of the library, its heavy stacks of books all in an order that scholars had figured out for organizing ideas. "You're paying for something you don't want."

"Basically," she said. She looked me in the eyes. "I'm here because I don't want to be homeless."

"There are options between flunking out and homelessness," I said.

"Maybe," she said. "But I don't know what they are."

That's a scene. Something is happening. Characters are involved. They are discussing a problem, smelling the atomic decline of old papers, hearing the door to a stairwell clicking shut, tasting salt on lips, tucking pencils into bookbags.

The opposite of showing is *telling*. If you write "I ran from the human world," that is telling, even though the sentence includes an action verb, "ran." In order to make this *showing*, a writer needs to say exactly how she ran from the human world. We need literality. "On the spring equinox I loaded a wheelbarrow with camping gear and ran it to the creek at the edge of my mother's property." There. That's you running from the world.

Focus on real-life scenes. Try to be in a sensible moment, in the sensate world, in your sensual body. Keep feeling, looking around, experiencing.

Also, be careful of confusing the virtual world with the real one. Once I had an undergraduate student who wrote an essay that consisted in huge part of text messages. She was writing about the singular and paralyzing loneliness of her childhood, when she looked for sisterhood, or siblinghood, everywhere, even in the most unlikely of places, the computer. She professed a storybook happiness with a virtual sisterhood she'd found. Most of her scenes consisted of multiple girls messaging each other. In this case her eyes were useless except for reading a blue-lit screen, the ears were useless except for the dings of notifications, the nose was useless except for ancillary smells, outside the story. And so forth.

Through this student I understood that creating scenes is difficult when a writer is describing computer-based relationships. "Maybe I'm not representative of a typical reader," I told her, "but I don't think people will be transported by a virtual life."

I remind you to print and hang the great Anton Chekhov quote above your writing desk. It has been summarized to this: "Don't tell me the moon is shining. Show me the glint of light on broken glass." Show, don't tell.

Remember that.

Another scene

Mama hears a noise. "I think someone's at the door," she says. I hop up off the sofa, where I've been lounging, although I really need to go home. This morning I sketched out six hours of brain-busting work, and I am getting none of it done.

I see someone standing outside the glass storm door. It's Faye, my ex-sister-in-law. Her hair is honey-brown and straight. She wears her usual walking shoes and carries a couple of foil-wrapped dishes. I hold the door wide for her.

"Wow!" I say. "I didn't expect you. Great to see you!" When the divorce happened, I thought that I might not see much of her, and that has proven to be the case. Now Mama has been diagnosed with metastasized cancer, and Faye, ever thoughtful and helpful, is coming through the door.

"I thought I'd bring by some food," she says. "This is beef stew. And some cornbread." She lays a Tupperware container and a small cardboard box on the kitchen table. She touches the box. "I cooked it on top of the stove," she says. Then she opens the box to show a small piece missing. "I had to try it."

"To make sure!" I laugh. I've missed Faye.

"That's right," she says.

"This is so kind. Thank you. Do you have a minute? Can you come in and talk?"

She could, and she did. Later I understood how much I had missed her and always would.

Nine things about a scene

1. It has a purpose in the big story.
2. It has a point of view.
3. It has a setting.
4. It moves the story along.

5. It often contains dialogue.
6. It has characters.
7. It has a beginning, middle, and end.
8. It contains description.
9. It contains memorable images.

Words that may indicate a scene

- one (followed by a unit of time)
- once
- this
- particular
- now
- see, saw, seen

And a caveat

Scenes are optional in everything except drama. Even fiction can be sceneless. Plenty of great writers don't use scenes at all —philosophers like Emerson, for example, or stream-of-consciousness writers like Kerouac. So you get to decide. If you're writing for self-care or to process your life—not writing as a professional, in other words—you can write however you like. There are no rules.

If, however, you want to get published, be widely read, join the body of literature-makers and culture-creators, and make money, then learn to write in scene.

Reflection, or telling

is the second basic element of prose. Reflection means the heady generalizations and abstractions and conceptualizations and woolgathering that we all write to process our thoughts and feelings. Kittredge was very hard on reflection. He called it our "bullshit."

Maybe that's too harsh, because reflection in a piece of writing is a signpost directing a reader to a path. If a scene were presented alone, the reader would wonder why—a scene has to have significance—and the writer shows this via reflection. A writer tells a reader why some particular scene has significance for them. Reflection is what you think about what's happening.

Understand, then: reflection is necessary. But most writers gorge on it. We love giving commentary and analysis.

The best method of writing a narrative (in my not-humble opinion) is to tell the story and let it speak for itself, and you as the narrator keep *your* opinions quiet, so that readers can form their own.

To the writer, commentary simply seems like writing. To the reader, it's telling, analysis, and personal opinion, which are things that a person wants only in small doses. Anybody starts to squirm when being told what to think.

Here's reflection copied from my journal.

> Little did I know how imperfect I would always feel, my clothes too tight, my little finger too crooked. My hair too gray, too chopped, too wispy, too scattered. My heart too fragile, like a bruised fruit, the old boyfriend telling me that I'd cry at a leaf's falling. And I would, I know I would, if the leaf had touched something inside me, if it were beautiful enough to scar me.

I'd like to say that nothing is happening here. But something *is* happening. It's all internal. It's me talking about how I'm feeling. It doesn't have the "weight" and "extension" of the tangible world that O'Connor talks about when she writes, "The fiction writer has to realize that he can't create compassion with compassion, or emotion with emotion, or thought with thought. He has to provide all these things with a body; he has to create a world with weight and extension."

Think of a lengthwise cross-section of a tree showing a line for the ground, with trunk and branches above, roots below. Scenes are the part above ground. Reflection is what's below.

More reflection

An alcohol addiction will rob you of everything until it takes your life. My brother died of it.

Or:

Bryce Canyon was my favorite.

Or:

I will always be his mother, but I cannot be the same mother I was. He will always be my son but not the same one.

Summary

is the third basic element of prose. When I say "summary" I don't mean the condensation of meaning. I mean summary that compresses time and lets the reader know what happens between one scene and the next. Madison Smartt Bell, in his book *Narrative Design*, calls it "an efficient account of events in a narrative that are not given full dramatic rendering."

Not everything can be put in scene. If you try to record every scenic moment of your day, or even a specific part of your existence, you become one of the obsessive-compulsive people whose life is record-making. To live completely in the present moment and also report on it is impossible. The solution is to summarize.

Summary can also condense reflection.

I once edited a memoir about a woman's experiences with native spirituality. Like most of us, she wanted to cast her net wide and talk about childhood, family, a failed marriage, and many other things that didn't directly move her main story along. My advice to her, and to you, is not to summarize the main thread of your story. Tell that in scenes (and I'd start with the scenes in chronological order). Summarize most everything else.

Summary doesn't have to be pedestrian. In *Narrative Design* Bell writes that summary can be written "winningly, persuasively, and beautifully." You may need less summary than you think. Bell talks about the "jump cut" of the movie industry. The jump cut is the break that allows a filmmaker or a writer to leap between scenes, more or less without transitions, and it assumes that the theater-goer or the reader is smart and will be able to follow your leap, and in fact is more intrigued *because* of that leap.

Here is an example of summary:

The months passed.

Another example:

Yesterday, and for the past few days, I've worked hours at my desk, which is the kitchen table these days. Almost all the work is on the computer.

One more example

I remember so many graveyards with my mother and father. One had a moldy concrete tree for a monument. One had words handwritten in homemade concrete, one had a child's marker, broken with a bat. Some were Black, some were White, one was an infant grave in a private family cemetery. Many were falling in, neglected, the way we neglect the dead, our ancestors.

Exercise

Go find an essay to read or reread. Circle all the scenes. Underline the abstraction. Highlight all places that summarize.

Prompt

1. Usually during the summer my family...(summary)
2. Summer to me was a time of...(reflection)
3. This particular summer day...(scene)

14

THWARTS

S tructure is how a writer combines the three elements— scene, reflection, and summary. Structure is a skeleton, a chassis, studs and trusses, a form that is sometimes created and sometimes unearthed. Years went by before I knew structure to be important. Now I think about it incessantly.

Kittredge's schema

I was a student in Bill Kittredge's nonfiction workshop at the University of Montana when I began to understand structure. In our first session nobody knew how to write an essay. "I didn't know how to write an essay either," he said. "I learned it from Terry McDonell."

The way Kittredge told it, McDonell was editing *Rocky Mountain* magazine when he phoned Bill to ask him to write an essay. McDonell would go on to lead *Rolling Stone, Newsweek, Esquire, Sports Illustrated,* and more. He is co-founder of the online magazine *Literary Hub.*

"I'd be glad to do it but I don't know *how* to write an essay," Kittredge told McDonell.

"I'll tell you how," McDonell said.

Years later, in 2016, when McDonell's memoir about being an editor, *The Accidental Life: An Editor's Notes on Writing and Writers*, came out, reporter Renee Montagne interviewed him for National Public Radio. Montagne, in introducing McDonell, said, "He enticed literary greats, many of them novelists, to write long-form pieces for his publications. He picked writers who lived as colorfully as they wrote and had an appetite for adventure far beyond their writing desks." Kittredge was one of these literary greats.

What Kittredge credits to McDonell became a formula taught to hundreds of writing students. I say "credits" because, after McDonell's book came out, I wrote asking him about the schema. He had no memory of ever outlining this to Kittredge. Here's what he said.

> Thank you for the kind words. I don't remember that call with Bill about "Redneck Secrets" as well as he does. I think I was just trying to get him to start thinking about the idea by asking for anecdotes and he filled in the rest. He's a great writer, as you know. So too Tom McGuane for that kind of piece. Take a look at his "An Outside Chance" collection. Thank you again for your interest.
>
> My best regards,
> Terry

This schema is what Kittredge taught me, and I'm going to share it with you. Please note that the formula names only two parts of prose—scene and reflection—instead of the three I insist on. I suppose, since I never thought to ask until too late, that Kittredge considered summary to be wrapped into the other two parts.

Here it is

First, write a 3- to 4-page anecdote with dialogue. This is a scene. It doesn't have to be connected to anything," Kittredge said. "There should be no argument at all." (I've learned a great way to do this, which I'll talk about soon. Hang with me.)

A scene can be any length.

Then, string a number of these anecdotes—seven of them, for example—together in such a way that they form a narrative arc. He told us that the number of scenes should be odd. Narrative arc is vital to this formula, and we'll explore that later. "It works just like a short story," Kittredge said.

Whatever your odd number, the middle scene in a traditional narrative arc would be the epiphanic scene. If you have seven, the fourth one is the recognition scene. The fifth is consequences. This leaves an equal amount of room for rising action on the front end and falling action on the back.

Begin each scene with reflection, your bullshit. That's the *telling*. "There are going to be moments," Kittredge said, "when you have to explain a scene. Tell us why it affects you." He told us to lay it at the beginning of a scene, no more than a few lines, although I've learned that it can go anywhere in the scene. This *tells* us what the scene is about. The scene itself, which follows the bullshit, is the *showing*.

The essay, then, is predominantly scenic. Humans are animals, living in an animal body, embodied. This is not living in the abstract. A scene is our animal life.

In this pattern, back and forth, abstraction introduces showing.

Furthermore

If you collect all the reflection from the beginning of each scene, those sentences compiled could summarize the entire essay. As Kittredge said it, "You could take all the abstract out of the essay and make a 1.5-page piece without the anecdotes that says everything. That's a good exercise."

When I'm teaching, I draw this out on a board, here outlined with five scenes.

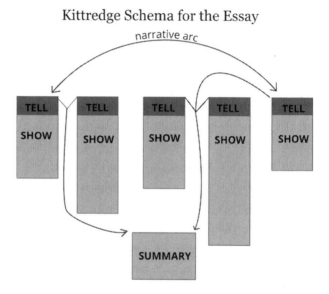

Kittredge Schema for the Essay

The epic beauty of this formula is that it forces a writer to work in scenes and to realize that underneath every powerful piece of writing lies a structural foundation.

90/10

In terms of proportions, Kittredge laid out a mathematical formula. He told his students—and I'm telling you exactly what he told me and Andrew Sean Greer and Amanda Eyre Ward (both in my class) and so many others. *Showing* should comprise about 90 percent of the finished piece, leaving 10 percent for *telling*.

Kittredge, as far as I can find, has never written about this schema. I'm presenting it as it was given to me.

500/200

Lucky for me, writer Philip Connors captured the same story I've just told in his 2002 article, "Not So Pretty Horses, Too." I say "lucky" because his article proves that I'm not making this stuff up. Connors did not actually study with Kittredge. A friend relayed to Connors what he had learned in a class with Kittredge, and Connors wrote about it.

Connors writes, "Thankfully, in 1978, Terry McDonell asked Kittredge to write an essay on the theme of 'redneck secrets.' Kittredge said he had no idea how to write an essay."

Connors continues, "A friend who sat in one of Kittredge's writing workshops at the University of Montana told me that Kittredge recounted McDonell's advice this way: Give me five scenes or anecdotes strung together with your own bullshit philosophy. Five hundred words of anecdote, 200 of your own bullshit, scene, bullshit, leading to a summation or revelation. It's that easy."

You see, then, that Connors transcribed the schema differently than I. As he described it, Kittredge's formula goes back and forth, alternating scene and reflection, 500/200 in words, or about 70/30 in percentages.

Perhaps Kittredge refined his formula as time passed, but the version he told me, in percentages, was 10, 90, 10, 90, 10, 90...and so on.

Like this

A few days after their conversation, Kittredge received from McDonell a copy of Larry McMurtry's "Take My Saddle from the Wall" (published in *Harper's* in 1968) with a two-word note attached.

"Like this," it said.

I had to go into the microfilm at Hollins University, where I was teaching, to find McMurtry's essay. I read it closely and I didn't see a formula there. I read Kittredge's redneck essay too, and I didn't see a formula in that essay either. Kittredge wrote, "A Redneck pounding a hippie in a dark barroom is embarrassing because we see the cowardice. What he wants to hit is a banker in broad daylight."

That is telling. Not showing.

Who knows? Perhaps Kittredge himself took years to figure out the schema. Perhaps the schema doesn't actually work. Perhaps it's meant to teach the beginning CNF writer something important. Perhaps following it is too formulaic, too difficult. No matter. Kittredge taught me this formula for essay-writing, and it woke something in me. That one schema made all the difference between me piddling and me publishing.

Now you have it. Try it out. Go make a ruckus with it.

The fraction is not 1/3

What is obvious to me now, 20-some years after I left the university, is that a portion of the *showing* has to be summarized, which makes it *telling without analysis*. In other words, the scene itself requires summary, and sometimes the reflection does too.

Therefore I take the liberty of revising Kittredge's schema to include three parts instead of two: reflection and scene, mixed with summary. There is no order. Any of this can fall anywhere. If we redo the math, it could look like 80 percent scene, 10 percent reflection, and 10 percent summary. Or, perhaps, 70, 15, 15.

The long and short of my advice is to focus on scenes, unless you're Ralph Waldo Emerson or Roxane Gay. Do *a lot* of showing and *a little bit* of summarizing and *a smidgen* of reflecting.

Of course, as we all hear endlessly, all rules in writing are made to be broken. So shatter them. I am not even telling you to understand the rules before you trash them. Many renegade and ground-breaking writers—Emily Dickinson, Chinua Achebe, Leslie Marmon Silko, and Jack Kerouac, for instance— have hatched experimental forms by following some wild hunch in their heads. Go do it. Impress us. Change us.

Mountain and sea

In a fascinating article called "A Narrative Logic of the Personal Essay," which published in the March/April 2018 issue of *The Writer's Chronicle*, writing professor Bruce Ballenger mapped almost scientifically a sheaf of essays to show the movement between narration (showing) and reflection (abstraction.) His metaphor is a "sea of experience" in which we swim and a "mountain of reflection" from "where it's possible to see patterns."

Ballenger found no rules for structure. Some very fine essays contain only brief moments of reflection; other very fine essays contain only brief moments of scene narration. That means you have no rules to live by. You can make your own.

I, however, am a trudger who learns by painstaking thought-experiment and practice. I would not have understood story had it not been for William Kittredge and his schema. That was the screwdriver with which I could deconstruct creative nonfiction and learn to write it.

You do what you want with this. It's yours. But I dare you to try it, at least once. I dare you to assume you can do it.

Narrative arc

Scenes should link to form a narrative arc. Let's talk about that.

The symbolic narrative arc classically looks like a Bell curve, with the first third of the line climbing. This represents a supply of information and build-up of tension. The apex of the curve is the climax, or epiphany, or recognition. The downward line symbolizes the unwinding, or *denouement*, which means "outcome" or "conclusion."

This model mirrors a five-part pattern of drama employed by Shakespeare and early dramatists—exposition, rising action, climax, falling action, resolution. (By the way, a brilliant explanation of narrative arc can be found in Madison Smartt Bell's *Narrative Design*. His model is triangular.)

Once I began to study structure, I realized that almost nothing I read fell into the perfect Bell-curve pattern of narrative arc.

For one thing, epiphanies happen not once in an essay but in every scene, usually multiple times, and so the arch should more aptly be a wavy not a straight line, each rise indicating an epiphany. It should be actually *very* wavy.

The main epiphany almost *never* happens in the exact center of the timeline. For me it mostly happens about two-thirds of the way into the story. For some reason, modern unwinding is shorter, maybe because we are dumber than Elizabethan theater-goers, requiring more time on the front end to understand a situation. Maybe we're addicted to tension. Maybe, once we understand a thing, we get out faster. Maybe we're less patient.

Some pieces, I've learned, lack *denouement* altogether. In nature writing especially, a writer may present a problem for which no solution has been reached. This requires code-breaking, and is why so many texts on environmental themes must rely on an interior landscape in which a transformation inside the writer becomes the epiphany.

In a course I drew the Kittredge schema out for folks to see. One of the writers in the class, Laura M. Terry, created a graphic for me that shows the arc's possibilities.

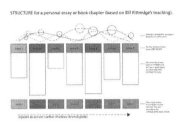

STRUCTURE for a personal essay or book chapter (based on Bill Kittredge's teaching).

Driving line

Before you write, should you know what you want to say? Or not know?

Writers usually sit solidly on one side of a line demarcating whether you should decide what you're going to say beforehand or wait for your muse to disclose these secrets.

The answer for me is both.

Let me attempt to convince you of the necessity for both logic and illogic.

In order for you, the writer, to construct an elegant narrative arc, you will need to understand a work's mission. For nonfiction, mission means a driving line, something you want or need to say. From the grandness of a book to the brevity of a flash essay, your nonfiction piece needs a driving line. (For fiction, that means a basic plot driven by some sort of emotional reckoning.)

Without a driving line, a writer can become a hoarder. She heaps stuff into a safety deposit box even when the material belongs in the trash. Annie Dillard said the hardest decision in writing nonfiction is "what to put in and what to leave out."

Or a writer can become a rabbit-chaser. He keeps going off on tangents, meaning instead of following a trail he set out on, he sidles off on down various side-trails, pursuing bunnies.

Or a writer can end up rendering a "situation" and not a "story."

Situation versus story

Let's talk a minute about the difference. Vivian Gornick, in her book *The Situation and the Story,* writes: "The situation is the context or circumstance, sometimes the plot...The story is the emotional experience that preoccupies the writer: the insight, the wisdom, the thing one has come to say." Bruce Ballenger expands on this idea in his piece "A Narrative Logic of the Personal Essay." He says, "It's never enough to simply have events to write about. It is in the examination of the reasons for and the consequences of the things that happen to us that give rise to stories."

If you don't plan ahead, you could very easily mistake a situation for a story.

Like it or not, nonfiction has a controlling idea. Everything should bow to the story's central "so what." A writer doesn't take a reader down a path and then say, *Oh sorry, there's nothing to see here after all.* Nailing that central point, to yourself, makes the whole journey worthwhile and easier.

Once that driving line—the emotional experience that leads to transformation, the insight, the wisdom, the thing you have come to say—is clear to you, you can then allow the illogical muse, the roving artist, and the word-wise coyote to lead you into myth and mystery.

So ask yourself: Can I name my idea straightforwardly, in two or three sentences?

If so—that, my friends, is your driving line.

Then light a candle, excuse the sage and invite the magician, and write the story.

What to include

A writer's first challenge is to decide the nature of an overarching mission for your story. Even a memoir needs this. A memoir is about your life, yes, but it also carries a weight that others feel in their lives. It will need common ground. Then you get to decide what to include.

You know you want to plant a garden in your yard, and you get to decide which plants to put in it. You'll want to choose the ones that belong to your region, and thus belong to you.

From that massive list, which do you include?

All of the plants from which you can choose are like your stories. You have thousands and thousands to choose from. Maybe this is going to be a pollinator garden using native plants. Or a food forest. Or vegetables.

You've narrowed down your choices.

Likewise, you winnow your stories down to a type.

Let's say you're going to write a spiritual memoir. Or an environmental text. Or a book about a single canoe trip down the Missouri River. Or the 10 years of your life where you lived on a commune.

Stick to the stories that pertain to that subject. Then hold nothing back. Spend all you've got.

Arrangement

To write an essay, a writer begins to collect ideas, dreams, memories, scientific research, scenes, and images about a topic that is of utmost importance to them. It's good to sit comfortably within your obsessions.

Then you'll need a structure, an order. Order means the sequence in which we narrate the parts of an essay to create arrangement.

While sifting through your collection of material about a chosen subject, the question becomes, as Alan Weisman, author of *The World Without Us* and many other fine books, first said to me, "What is the story? What does it mean? Why is it important? What am I trying to say?"

Then you figure out the most appealing and artful way to say it.

Often you start writing before you figure out the "most appealing and artful way." That's good. Don't sit and wait. Just get started. If you get stuck, do some flow-writes: *What I'm trying to say is...*or *What I want to say about this is...*

Find an order. Reorder. Reorder again.

Many metaphors come to my mind with arrangement. I think of a train moving down a track—which car goes first and which goes next, how they get arranged, how the engine is so powerful and how we all love that mineral-red caboose signaling the end.

In terms of metaphor I think too of constructing a hiking trail in a wood—you flag a trailhead and think about landmarks a hiker would want to experience, and decide where to bring the hiker out of the woods, maybe on the opposite side of a parking lot. Essentially this means

- where you start,
- where you go,
- where you come out.

The thread

My favorite metaphor for order involves a feed sack. When you live on a farm, you open lots of these unless you grow your own animal feed. Feed sacks are stitched closed with thick cotton thread in an intricate weave, and the factory leaves the thread-ends dangling. If a farmer pulls most any of the loose thread-ends, it will tighten into a knot. However, one thread will not tighten but will unravel beautifully and open the bag. Usually I don't find it and I wind up hauling out a pocketknife and slicing open the bag. If I am lucky enough to recognize and pull the magic thread, then with one quick zip a bag of golden grain lies waiting.

That's what happens with story. You work your way through your collection of ideas, dreams, memories, scientific research, scenes, and images. You begin to write, or to unzip the thread. If a knot begins to form, you try another thread. One of them is going to work.

You have to find the one magic thread.

I like to start an essay with an anecdote, as Kittredge taught. A scene right at the beginning makes your piece come alive, and hopefully inspires you to work more in scene (showing) and less in abstraction (telling).

But that's optional. Writer Holly Haworth has a gorgeous essay, "A Return to Feeling," in the 2023 anthology *Solastalgia* (University of Virginia Press, edited by Paul Bogard) that relies on a couple of very short scenes but that is mostly deep-time reflection on eco-grief. She begins with the idea of feeling. She stirs around the multiple meanings of the word. Finally she picks up the theme of hands, how useful our hands have been to us, and ends with her driving line: How we move forward through the climate crisis is by us feeling our way ahead. "I think we could feel our way forward like this, in the darkness, through the disappearances." Hers is a beautiful and inspiring essay. I cite "A Return to Feeling" to give you an example of how one genius writer took a collection of material sewed shut and opened it into a bag of golden grains.

Ask yourself, "What is my main mission or thesis with this piece and how can I arrange the material to fit an arc reaching recognition and awareness?"

Finding the thread

When I was writing *Ecology*, I would spread chapters on the floor, trying to find the thread. The process was so new to me and so frustrating, and my brainpower so weak, that I'd start crying. I mean, I'd *weep*.

I didn't figure out the structure of *Ecology*, in the end. I signed with Milkweed Editions, and Emilie Buchwald, founder, publisher, and my visionary editor, took the manuscript on a two-week vacation, where she figured out a structure. She instructed me to start with birth, end with leaving Georgia, and alternate the chapters, personal history then natural history, humans and nature, back and forth.

As we worked together, Buchwald tasked me with creating a timeline of events. She wanted to understand when things were happening and make sure I was presenting information sequentially in the text. Since then, I have often created time-lines when working with a body of material, and I have created genealogies and lists of characters and maps and whatever other supporting material helps dog a story along. A reader often never sees these supporting documents but they keep a writer on point.

Perhaps you can find such a dedicated and genius editor as Buchwald, but I can tell you that they are increasingly difficult to find. Most editors don't have the time or wherewithal or experience to shape books for writers. They're looking for easy pickings, and you as creative genius have to make a book ripe and ready for them.

Outlines

A few years ago I accepted an invitation to serve on a dissertation committee for a brilliant guy who found writing very difficult. His dissertation, which he desired to turn into a popular book on sustainable farming, suffered from lack of an outline. He knew what he wanted to say, and he had done months of research, but his ideas were jumbled on all levels. Not only sentences and paragraphs but entire pages were out of place.

For example, all of the following ideas, a sentence or two devoted to each, occurred in *one small paragraph.*

- human connection to food
- farmers as expendable
- destruction of local economies
- industrialization
- spiritual separation from nature.

The paragraph made no logical sense, as if every thought was a non sequitur. *It does not follow.*

The subjects were interrelated, yes. So is all of life. So what? A reader needs to understand what you are trying to say. Otherwise, what's the point of writing?

Creative nonfiction writers have to resist the urge to talk in circles. You know how much I, being a poet and a wild woman, am opposed to linearity, but I have to admit that, in order to be well understood, writing in a linear fashion—subject after subject, story after story, so that a reader can follow our thinking—is the way to go.

We open a feed sack. We lead a reader down a trail. We put a train on a track.

"My advice to you," I told my friend, "is to create a viable outline, not simply with chapter titles but with extensive listings under each chapter heading. Then use a pair of scissors to cut each page apart and re-form pages under appropriate headings. You have to write this in a more-systematic, less-random manner, or this manuscript is going to stay a jumbled mess, and you'll stay confused and undirected. You shouldn't do anything more here until you get the structure correct."

Writing is hard work. It takes tremendous brainpower. It makes you crazy, it makes you want to scream.

I'm not going to speak to fiction or poetry, because they are different beasts. For creative nonfiction, if the structure is sound, the writing gets much, much easier.

And so you don't worry about him, the candidate got his PhD.

Organizing your material

When you're working with a mountain of material, you have one major practical problem. Your brain is not a computer. It is not large enough, not normally, to arrange all the files and studies and references and flow-writes and ideas and drafts you've collected, especially for 250 pages of a book.

Therefore, how do you organize and arrange the pieces?

A superfluity of "stuff" in general has caused a need for information about organizing our homes, our closets, and our lives, which has inspired entire corporations, books, podcasts, magazines, and more.

With a longer writing project, the stuff is important. You need to collect and keep all the parts you can find. The principles for organizing the material are similar to those for Marie Kondoing your home.

Create a system of dividing the material into manageable parts. Organize by chapters, by subject, by month—whatever makes sense. Make and label digital folders for categories and subcategories.

Put like items together.

Declutter, if possible. I make a folder marked "Peripheral" or "Maybe" for the iffy material.

Train yourself to store info in its correct folder once you collect it.

Many apps have been developed for the sole purpose of solving this problem. Scrivener is best known, and it promises to "help you organize long writing projects such as novels, nonfiction books, academic papers, and even scripts." In addition, there's Chapterly, LivingWriter, Milanote, and probably many more.

I resist forces determined to computerize my life, and I hold out for the analog as long as humanly possible. For example, I purchased a mobile phone in the early 2020s, and we barely have cell service in the out-of-the-way place we happily live. Therefore, I am not a subscriber to online writing organizers. Not yet.

Three-dimensions

For John McPhee the folder was a literal folder into which all material on a specific topic went. When he began to write a chapter, he took out that folder only. He writes lovingly about this in his book on writing, *Draft No. 4*.

Some writers use note cards flipped out across a table.

Some clip index cards to a clothesline or pin them to a wall.

Kittredge said to put 3x5 cards on a corkboard. "Keep staring at them. Keep reordering things," he said.

Similarly, Robert Olen Butler in *From Where You Dream: The Process of Writing Fiction*—lectures compiled and edited by novelist Janet Burroway—lobbies for a system of index cards that get shuffled and reshuffled.

Some writers type and print out pieces, arrange them on a bare floor in a logical, workable order, then clip them together.

Some tape scraps of paper together.

Faulkner's study has an outline for *A Fable* (1954) still readable in pencil on ivory-painted walls.

One of my favorite stories about arrangement came from Kittredge, who told me about a guy who wrote in a derelict Missoula hotel that was scheduled for demolition. The guy set up his typewriter in an empty room and scribbled outlines on the walls. When one room was filled, he moved to another. Although the story sounds like an urban myth, Kittredge swore it was truth. That guy happened to be a novelist, but for a nonfiction writer outlining is even more important. It will save your writing life.

If you're not sure what to include

I suggest a flow-write. Set a timer for five minutes and keep your pen moving, as Natalie Goldberg advises, starting with this prompt, "What I want to write about is....."

This will be your driving line or your controlling idea—what the story is about. What you include will be the memories, scenes, dreams, reflections, images, and facts that further this vision.

The anecdotes drive the line.

Eliminate scenes and bits that don't further your controlling idea and while doing so discover more parts that do.

How do you pick scenes?

Once an interviewer asked me, "How did you pick and choose memories from childhood to write *Ecology of a Cracker Childhood*?"

I tried to pick those anecdotes and memories that would pertain to my main theme or drive my line—in this case the human relationship with nature, or more aptly, how the culture of southern-coastal-plains folk is bound to the ecosystem of longleaf pine.

I needed pieces that would move *that particular story* forward.

The scenes had to be interesting and lively. They had to be, in other words, scenic. I couldn't blather on too much about my ideas or thoughts or abstractions. I had to have people moving around, doing things, saying things, smelling liatris in bloom, hearing bobwhites call.

Some of the stories were not my actual memories. I interviewed a lot of people, especially family members, for the book, so some of the stories were other people's memories. But the rule was, the anecdote couldn't go into the book unless it drove the line.

Do you winnow and weed stories?

Heck to the no. Write everything down at first. Just get started. Later you can decide what your story is about, what to include, and what to quietly slip into a file for later use. Or into the trash can.

Time

I want to speak with you about a small and prudent matter, about where to begin a story.

An axle on which every story in the world turns is time. Time must be managed, like a flock of sheep, or it will run away from you.

The story is complicated. It's a long story that goes back a long way. You agonize over where to begin it, how to tell it. In what order should your material go?

Should you start at the end and tell the story all the way back to the beginning? Should you start someplace in the middle? Should you spiral, meander, coil, stack, weave? Should you flash back? Should you imbed a flashback within a flashback?

Should you start in one place and then reverse into some backstory? Oh my gosh, we love backstory. "Let me explain how I got here."

Please note this. *The order that is most understandable to a reader and to a writer is chronological.*

Chronology

We writers, of course, want to do fancy pirouettes and leaps, so we jump back and forth and up and down, exhibiting our gymnastic abilities. We do a handstand across the gunwale.

However. If you want to be understood, if you're writing to make a difference, if you want a narrative that hits the reader in the gut because it's constructed the way we all think, consider simplifying. Following chronological order. At least at first.

Benjamin Percy said in his book *Thrill Me* that when his students ask how much backstory to put in, he says, "How about none?" If backstory is absolutely necessary, drop it in slowly. Stay in the scene but dole out small pieces of history, in the same way you don't flood a reader with description but mete that out.

There are actually, however, *two* chronological orders.

One is the bona fide order of events.

The other is the private chronological order of your protagonist (which can be you) coming to understand.

So there.

When you are writing a story chronologically, start with a single point farther back in time and move toward another, more-recent point in time. Everything that happens before your starting moment is in the past and should be treated as such, and everything that happens after your final moment is in the future and should be treated accordingly. You can write in whatever verb tense you want.

Simple, I know, but you wouldn't believe how many people don't get this.

When I turned in my first draft of *Ecology of a Cracker Childhood*, it was all over the place time-wise. My editor, Emilie Buchwald, had me go through the book and put a date on everything that happened: 1962, 1969, 1970. Then I had to rearrange the. entire. thing. into chronological order. She said, "Start when you were born and end when you left Georgia." I followed her guidance and that made for a better book. So do it.

Sketch your story out for yourself, horizontally. Your opening scene comes first. Name that point in time. Name what's next, and next. Skip some space and name the scene where you are ending. You are starting with a strange perfume on a shirt and ending with turning a key to a new home in Hawaii. You are starting with a cancer diagnosis and ending with a moment in the garden at sunset. You are starting with getting fired from the old job and ending with picking up *The New York Times* and seeing your name on the bestseller list.

You get the picture.

Where to begin? At the beginning. The true beginning. The point where everything that came before is extraneous. But everything that came after is life and death.

Other structures

I like the Kittredge schema because it teaches a new writer what's necessary to know. But it's one of many. Chronology of time or of understanding, or some experimental order, can operate within any structural form.

- visitation
- journey
- self-defense
- rescue
- unit or units of time—a day in the life of, months, seasons
- classic fairy tale (a hero, a crime, a victim, a villain)
- story within a story
- flashback
- alternation of points of view
- cycles through multiple points of view
- alternation of past and present
- alternation of internal story with external story
- stream of consciousness
- hodge-podge

I highly recommend reading the first two chapters in John McPhee's *Draft No. 4*. One chapter is called "Progression" and the other "Structure." McPhee crazily draws out mind-blowing spirals, uphill lines hanging with boxes, and planets orbiting a sun as the models for his essays. The book is worth obtaining and studying.

I once sat in on an hour-long workshop at a writing festival at the University of Alabama with environmental writer David Gessner. I was surprised to realize, at the end of his class, that he too had offered a schema. Gessner's was simplified, no doubt, considering the duration of the class, although he intended for each participant to have a mini-essay by the end of an hour. The structure had four parts and Gessner accompanied each section with an adroit cartoon on a whiteboard.

A. Enter a place. B. Enter the physical world. C. Write a scene. D. Find meaning in it. Gessner drew a stick figure spewing thoughts, then three pottery vessels floating in air, or "the shapes the spew can take." "Ask for some bigness," Gessner said.

Another couple of thoughts

I don't want to add more pain or woundedness to the world. Every scene I include gets evaluated for potential pain it could cause. Sometimes I use it anyway, if the benefit is greater than the loss. Any scene that will cause unnecessary division or hatred I discard.

I try not to single anyone out. I more often opt for systemic oppressions rather than individual ones.

I often change names when a scene will implicate someone rightly or wrongly, and when the implication doesn't justify the potential harm. I don't like to burn bridges. You get to decide this, of course. Tons of memoirists burn lots of bridges, and we live in a culture that likes to cancel people. That's a last resort for me.

Transitions

A piece starts to fall apart if it contains too many disparate stories strung together with the flimsiest of driving lines. The writer of such a piece is obligated to re-read it with an eye toward which stories are most important to the narrative and which are dispensable, and cut some of the less integral ones. The problem becomes transition, or writing strong enough transitions that the stories seem to belong together, and in fact, cannot be imagined anywhere else. One thing has to follow into the next, naturally, without force or effort.

Some leaping is tantalizing. But too many leaps too quickly, for no good and apparent reason, will jettison a good reader, as well as cause your work to lose direction, to wander, to flounder.

The question becomes, what does all this add up to?

Once I offered to edit a friend's essay about growing up in a potent and colorful time, San Francisco in the eighties. The essay wasn't working, according to my friend, who is a glorious writer and already had published two or three award-winning books. She had an interesting childhood in a hip place, and I thought she could spin that to gold.

She was right that the essay didn't work. It was not working to the extent that I, who need this advice myself on a daily basis, couldn't brainstorm any way to redeem it, and I advised her to stick it away in a drawer and to rob ideas and even paragraphs from it, but not try to salvage it. I told her that I spend my time moving forward, chalking irredeemable stuff up to practice.

"Your problem is not subject matter," I told her. "Your problem is lack of a through-line, of a narrative thread. The essay isn't enough about any one thing to actually have a structure. The important thing here really—the only thing—is your coming of age, and that story gets lost."

The opportunity to read my friend's essay provided me with a wonderful metaphor, that a driving line is to a piece of writing as a queen is to a beehive. At that moment on the farm where I live and write, I happened to have a queenless hive. Without a queen a hive cannot survive. The queen had died for unknown reason, and I had purchased another. The new queen was ensconced in the hive in a screen trap the size of a mint tin, and I was waiting on worker bees to eat out a sugar plug that confined her. The sugar plug was important. It represented time. By the time worker bees, mining through sugar, reached their new leader, they would have accepted her and wouldn't kill her. With a queen the hive could survive, because a queen provides direction, meaning, continuance.

Far too many essays suffer from not having a queen—not knowing what they are about, not having direction, not offering continuance.

Kittredge advised his students to tell a story in a straightforward but eloquent fashion. Put up road signs all over the place, he said, because people get confused. "Subtlety is not a virtue" were his exact words.

Title

Finally, craft a title for your piece that works as a big city-limits sign. "This is Portland."

Structure first

Part of being a writer is to give structure to formlessness, definition to the indeterminate, and precision to the approximate, even while remaining formless, indeterminate, and approximate. This seems insane, doesn't it?

But we do it. Every day.

Also

I have learned that when a piece is not coming together, structure is often the problem. Line edits are useless if structure isn't right.

This brings me to the end of what I have to say about structure.

∽

Exercise

Map out an essay using the Kittredge schema.

Prompt

I remember the exact day...

15

THE CURSE

I f writing, coming from the imaginal realm, is mythic—if writing is a charm of sorcery, witchery, and magic-making—then there has to be an evil eye. There is. There is a curse.

The "curse" of narrative is that the stripped-down, bare-bones story still tells the story. *This happened, then that happened, then that happened.* But that's often pedestrian, dull, and boring. To avoid this jinx means to bring into your employ a large number of literary techniques and devices that catapult nonfiction into literature.

I've been collecting a by-no-means-comprehensive list of ways to avoid the tyrannical dullness of pedestrian narrative.

Write toward your obsessions.

"Writing well is a matter of figuring out what obsesses you," Kittredge told me. "What obsesses you? Head toward your life's work."

Throughout our semester he kept repeating this maxim. "Work as close to your obsessions as you possibly can," he said.

Writer Kate Schimel remembered in her essay on Kittredge and storytelling in *High Country News* (Jan. 18, 2021) him saying: *Find your obsessions and follow them.*

When John McPhee talks about how he chooses his subjects, he says that a huge percentage are those he was interested in as a young person. The best passions start when we are young and remain with us throughout our lives.

I encourage writers in my workshops to brainstorm what they are passionate about. I set a timer for five minutes and ask them to make a list in their journals answering the question: *What obsesses me?*

To think that a writer needs a reference list of obsessions is absurd. However, a laborious brainstorm drives home this point: If a subject consumes you, inflames you, turns you into a geek, then, my sweetheart, your writing on the subject will reflect white-hot fire.

When I was first learning to write, I wrote what an editor wanted. This was back in the days when we had editors. I wrote about organizing closets and stocking ponds and hunting ghosts. At a certain point, long before I could afford to do so, I quit taking on such jobs. I wrote about things that obsessed *me*. I usually wrote without an assignment, which was financially risky and even financially dumb, hoping to find a publisher afterward. Thus many pieces I wrote did not publish. However, I can say this: When I enter my writing room, a little flame that eternally burns rises up and starts to really hiss. As an artist that's priceless.

Lots of people call themselves writers—cookbook writers, reporters, copywriters, ad writers, screenwriters. However, way out beyond the cul-de-sac at the end of the street you find the breed of writers who are magicians. They're trying to make doves disappear, or create smoke, or cause some soot-black cauldron to boil over, or entice a route of coyotes to dance senselessly. Those people are obsessed. Crazy.

Yeah.

That's the passion I'm talking about when I say *Write toward your obsessions*. Anything written toward your obsessions will automatically be better than anything written toward an editor's obsessions.

So be passionate.

Write toward your center.

Australian novelist Kim Mahood wrote a beautiful line in her essay "Listening is harder than you think," published in *The Griffith Review* (Issue: Re-Imagining Australia). The essay is about her return visits to an Aboriginal community where she lived as a child. "At least part of the motivation for these return journeys is the search for an authentic voice to tell the story lodged at the center of my preoccupations as an artist and a writer."

That line moves mountains. What story is lodged at the center of your preoccupations?

Work in scene.

I've written about this already.

Many people who have a desire to write and are honoring a deep impulse inside themselves at first have difficulty identifying a scene or even recognizing the difference between showing and telling. If you are one of these folks, no worries, because this isn't easy.

As I told a young writer I was editing, "The piece is nice until the walk with Katherine is over, and then the concrete ends and the abstract begins. The piece sits down and mutters to itself. We readers, on the other hand, want some breathing and odors and noises out in the kitchen."

Find metaphors.

The word "metaphor" comes from the Greek *meta*, meaning "over" and *pherin*, "to carry" or "to bear," including to bear children. To carry over. To carry one idea over to another. In writing, a metaphor is used to describe one thing as if it were another. It's an implied comparison, a bridge.

Metaphors have two parts, a tenor and a vehicle. The tenor is what is being described, and the vehicle is the language used to describe it. The tenor can be either a concrete or an abstract noun, as can the vehicle.

The best metaphors simplify an idea by making it accessible, meaning they compare one idea to something we easily understand in order to help us internalize it and accept it.

I've included a chapter on metaphors, coming up.

Describe stuff.

When you're writing, in any genre, describe a thing you're talking about. Allow a reader to see in their mind what you see in yours.

Work in concreteness (roses), not abstraction (love). Describe scenery, people, props, the built environment, the landscape. These details labor night and day on your behalf. Let description do its job.

I have heard said, of sketching: *The more you draw, the more you see. And the more you see, the more you draw.* The same is true of writing. And also true—the more you write, the better you write.

As Terry McDonell told NPR many years ago, "I think that what distinguishes the best writers is voice....(The writers I worked with) were completely different voices, but they were immersive, and they paid very close attention to detail so that you saw exactly what they were writing about."

He went on, "You never saw the word 'amazing' or 'unbelievable.' You saw specifics."

Flannery says, "Fiction operates through the senses" and "The first and most obvious characteristic of fiction is that it deals with reality through what can be seen, heard, smelt, tasted, and touched." Readers need to know what nouns—especially persons—look like. So use more concrete details.

Write about people.

Over the course of our correspondence, Alan Weisman gave me two "unbreakable" rules about writing. Number one, "Don't quit asking and researching until you know what the story really is and what it means to us. And number two, "Tell the story—any story—through living, breathing people."

I often come back to those two rules. I didn't understand them when they were given to me but I am starting to.

Describe the people.

Beginning writers often forget descriptions of people. For example, I tend to write about my husband, Raven. I drop his name everywhere, assuming everybody knows how Raven looks, how wolfishly green his eyes are and how he wears his hair long and wild. But *you* probably don't know how Raven looks.

So I have to describe him to you. "Raven's a tall, thin guy with a head shaped like Adonis who wears a shirt with holes in it when he's painting."

The writer knows what a certain person looks like. Describing that person to a stranger reading your work is not patently obvious.

Use memorable details.

Often in workshop I will ask a writer to read a piece aloud. Afterward I query the listeners, *What do you remember from that excerpt?* I ask such a question so the writer can learn what sticks in a reader's mind. Nine times out of 10 the listeners remember visuals, objects they were able to *imagine*, thus see—a leafless tree along a shallow brown river, a door falling off a red car, a hemp pull cord for a toilet in a cruise ship cabin. They don't remember the high-falutin' reflections. Nope, they don't. Sorry.

The test, then, for effective details is, Are they memorable? Did you *see* them and thus recall them so that the reader likewise can see them?

Train yourself to describe.

I want to add one more bit of information about showing. Description is a matter of training. I force myself, sometimes late in the writing process, to add lines of description. So. Go back through your writing during a revision and make sure that you have described all the things that a reader may actually and truly want to visualize.

Pay attention to images.

One exercise I started in grad school helped me learn to pay better attention to the world around me, and I want to share it with you.

You know how, as you're going about your day, you notice a small thing, something you see in your yard or on the street or at a shop. It may be a shirt someone is wearing, and the shirt has a botanical print. Or how unripe elderberries look when they are tiny and green.

These images get forgotten. But when you're writing they

are helpful in setting a stage, in showing a place, in describing a person. In grad school I realized that good writing needs to be filled with images—things people can *see*, meaning *imagine*, as they read the work.

In *Writing as a Sacred Path* author Jill Jepson shows why we need to train ourselves to really see. "A well-known Zen story tells of a famous teacher who asked his student if he'd been practicing awareness every minute. 'Yes!' the student answered enthusiastically. But when the teacher asked him if he'd placed his umbrella on the left or right side of his shoes when he entered the meditation hall, the student couldn't answer."

Try this exercise. At the end of the day or whenever you sit down to write, scan in your mind the preceding hours. What images stand out? These don't have to be major or pivotal. They don't need to be incorporated into your writing that day.

Jot them in the form of a list in your journal. Later, when you are writing about this period in your life, you glance back and see the small details already captured.

Here is a list of images from my journal. That day I had interviewed a man known as Captain Stan, a boat captain on the coast of Georgia.

- A long, low house still recognizable as a trailer home although it is sided with T-111 painted moss-green
- A brindle dog, part pit, that hustles down a sandy driveway toward me, tail wagging
- Knee-high rattlesnake boots that are muddy and worn
- A pound-sized bag of turmeric sitting upright on a kitchen counter
- A tall, stainless steel coffeepot in the style of a percolator

- The front door rigged on a spring so that two
  resident dogs can push in and out

That's it. Keep logs of images.

Avoid abstraction.

If you cannot recognize abstraction, get someone to mark it for you in a text you've written. Abstraction is everywhere, always beckoning to you from the treeline. Most of this is our so-called wisdom, what we think we know. Our bullshit wisdom. Say no.

Sometimes we try to use abstraction to create a mood or setting. No again. You cannot create silence by using the word "silence." Definitely you can't create silence by saying aloud that everything is silent. You create silence by quietly describing silent things.

You can't create love by saying it's love. Well, actually you can. But nobody will believe you.

Save word diversity.

When I was young and knew I wanted to write—actually, even before I knew—I became a student of words. I was a competitive speller. Besides the dictionary, I studied boxes of vocabulary intended for students to prepare for college entrance exams. I did crossword puzzles. I read books. I made lists of words.

I learned quickly that for every passion there exists an entire lexicon—one for sailing, one for cooking, one for woodworking. There is a nomenclature for color. One for the body. One for landscapes and natural phenomena. One for everything on earth. Science particularly has an unbelievably specific and particular language. Look at the names for every bone in the foot, for example.

This has proven vastly useful.

To a writer words are the atoms in a molecule, they are building blocks, they are Lincoln Logs or Legos. I like to think of words as minerals. Mostly we have granite, those well-worn rocks that pop up over and over: *be, and, of, a, in, to, have, too, it, I*. But some are beautiful, pink quartz, or rare, kyawthuite or an Ellensburg blue agate.

The diversity of language is in decline. We are, of course, losing entire languages. Kim Mahood talks about this in her essay "Listening is harder than you think." She writes about Bessie, an Aboriginal leader. "She is troubled too by the knowledge that she is the last fluent speaker of the local language in the community." Bessie wants to visit a special place, a lake that is important in her culture, so Mahood drives her. When they arrive Bessie approaches the shoreline, talking to the lake in her native tongue. Mahood writes, "When the invocation is finished she says, 'When I'm dead there'll be nobody left to talk to the lake in its own language.'"

Our personal vocabularies are in decline, as well. Somewhere I heard about a researcher who fed Shakespeare's published work into a computer program and figured out that Shakespeare's working vocabulary was about 30,000 words, depending on how they're counted. "Working" meant a word was used five or more times. I cannot find the exact study, so I'm hesitant to say much about this. Hemingway's vocabulary was a few thousand. The contraction of our collective vocabularies means the contraction of our personal vocabularies. Our language is shrinking. Kittredge thought that maybe this decline was a result of being lied to incessantly in our culture, that we were becoming suspicious of language itself.

Words possess a tremendous power. I want to know more of them. I want a working vocabulary that is larger, not smaller.

Collect words.

Above my writing desk I tack lists of words. One entire page is collectives: *a sloth of bears, a murder of crows, a crash of rhinoceri, a skulk of foxes, a rafter of turkeys, a gulp of cormorants.*

Another page contains synonyms of the color green.

Another is a page of odors.

If the language in a book is particularly vivid and embodied, I plunder it for lists. *Cold Mountain* was the first book from which I jotted down a vocabulary. Charles Frazier is a pro at finding and using lovely antique words, and on that particular list is *frabbled, cheroot, psalter, limned, hank, tablatorium,* and *sybaritic*, plus the amazing phrase *hawk-voiced prothalamion.*

I found a legendary frittery of words in *The Pat Conroy Cookbook.* Conroy developed an incredible vocabulary, a delicious glossary!—*rhomboids, seawater, horseradish, madcap, gravitas, almond-shaped, catlike.* Strange how even his cookbook lights up with strange life-forms of words.

Focus on action verbs.

Most of my word collections are action verbs in present tense harvested from my favorite books. A Cormac McCarthy novel started it. McCarthy is a master of simple but exact verbiage, and after I finished *All the Pretty Horses* I started a list. The very first sentence in the book reads, "The candleflame and the image of the candleflame caught in the pierglass twisted and righted when he entered the hall and again when he shut the door."

I wrote *twist, right, enter,* and *shut* to start my list. "Right" as a verb differs mightily from "right" as an abstract noun.

From *Cities of the Plain,* also by McCarthy, a book I consider a masterpiece, I have *lope, snatch, totter, seethe, scramble, brace, swivel, bolt, idle, snuff,* among many, many others. As I said, I have an entire page of action verbs in the present tense from this book.

Hanging before me as I write are handwritten pages full of words. *Loft, rein, shorten, snuff, yank, whittle, wrangle. Mold, cycle, lament, rattle, stagger, churn, swivel. Range, kindle, fawn, milk, trespass, kiss, gild, compound.* (Note that every one of those is a verb.)

Choose manifold functionality.

Many words serve multiple purposes in a language. Words that serve plural gods work doubletime and tripletime for you. For example, some are both nouns and verbs.

A churn, to churn

Snuff, to snuff

Milk, to milk

Some are homonyms, and using one evokes the other (flower, flour).

Some are two nouns at once (coffee the ground substance, coffee the cup of liquid).

Some have multiple and disparate meanings. A horse or a person can wear shoes, for example. Shell is both an outer garment and an outer layer of ocean creature. A corn kernel can be a kernel of truth.

Let word origins work for you.

Words that have their roots in Latin are generally different from those based in Angle and Saxon cultures.

Consider the word "axe." It's Anglo-Saxon, of Germanic origin. Such words like "axe" are:

- shorter
- more concrete
- often monosyllabic, blunt, or guttural

- informal
- often of the body
- often feelings-based

Now consider the word "pontificate." It's Latinate in origin, and such words, deriving from the Romance languages, are:

- longer
- more abstract
- often polysyllabic, or mellifluous
- more formal
- often of the mind
- often ideas-based

I teach these differences in my courses, because it's important to understand the layers and eons of meaning behind word choice. I do an exercise where I call out Latinate words. Very readily writers respond with Anglo-Saxon synonyms, proving that most of us have a gut understanding of etymology.

Masticate is Latinate. A Germanic equivalent would be *chew*.

Try it. *Inundate* is Latinate—what is its Germanic equivalent?

What about *consume*?

Imbibe?

Cogitate?

Consecrate?

Precipitation?

Inebriated?

Terminate?

Fallacious?

You get it.

Academic writing is heavy on Latinate words, which makes it feel erudite, elevated, dense, and more difficult to read. Creative writing is based in the body—in weight and extension, as Flannery would say—and Anglo-Saxon words, being of the body, generate more electricity for the writer.

Think about this when you're at your desk. Try to use words with punch.

However, Latinate words are often more lyrical and flowing than Anglo-Saxon ones. Therefore, I should say instead to be conscious of word choice in order to ensure a word is doing the job you're asking it to do. Don't fall into the quagmire of using Latinate words because you want to sound smart.

Consider indigenous words.

What I've learned is that not only do Anglo-Saxon words stand in sharp contrast to Latinate words, so do those of most native languages. I realized this after reading linguist Keith Basso's eye-opening book, *Wisdom Sits in Places: Landscape and Language Among the Western Apache*. Native words are in general

- more land-based.
- communal in essence.
- sensate.
- evocative of the mysterium.

On the other hand, Latinate words are

- based more heavily in built environments.
- geared more toward the individual.
- more insensate.
- biased toward science and reason.

We're losing native languages, native words, but if some are at your disposal and you can work to incorporate them in your writing, then why not.

Use words as resistance.

Some years ago the Oxford Junior Dictionary culled words that, as it turned out, were more indigenous than Latinate. Words that concerned nature, farming, food, and religion were falling out of favor, replaced by words belonging to our new vocabularies of technology. Suddenly *kingfisher* and *willow* and *otter* were gone, swapped for *broadband* and *database* and *analogue*.

One important implication of this change, as the British nature writer Robert Macfarlane wrote in *The Guardian*, is "A place literacy is leaving us." Not only is a place literacy leaving us, so is a language of human interaction, of community, of the senses, of symbolism, of myth. A literacy of mystery is leaving us.

Barry Lopez was keenly aware of this and wrote about it in his book *Home Ground: Language for an American Landscape*, a lexicon of place-words.

As I work with a manuscript, I keep replacing less interesting words for more unusual, real, active, and exact ones. I attempt to keep alive glossaries of place and wildness and bodies and food. I challenge myself to find novel ways to use the OJD deletions.

My advice to you: in an era of virtual chatrooms and facetimes and cell phones, focus on IRL—in real life--the chatroom of the kitchen and the facetime of the mirror.

Note "says."

Use a diversity of words, with one exception. *Says* is the best verb for someone speaking. We can spend a lot of time finding substitutes—*encourages, stresses, reveals*—but in most cases, *says* is best.

Expand your vocabulary.

To diversify your language, you have to pump your vocabulary iron. Words are like muscles—you have to use them, flex them, and stress them, or they will fail you. Study words. Keep reading. Read great writers. Read classics. Read the dictionary. Make lists.

Add more dialogue.

In general dialogue denotes a scene, so it's always a good thing. It's showing. Use it, except of course when more dialogue is not needed.

And make your dialogue interesting.

Nobody wants to hear endless talk about the weather over endless cups of coffee. We want drama, dammit.

Turn the rocks into gold.

I struck up a LinkedIn friendship with Rob Weinstein, comedy writer. One of my posts about writing and magic got him thinking. He wrote me this.

> Then, this morning, I was just doing what I always do: reading a book sentence by sentence looking for beautiful uses of words, and thought I'd suggest an exercise for your book.
> I'll call it, "Where is the magic? Where is the dross?"
> The author I was reading is Nigel Tranter.
> The dross was: Several cliched or over over-used descriptive words. Things along the lines of thunder booming, lightning flashing, sunshine slanting into a room, a knight's sword

clanging on contact. Describing facial features as an absolute indicator of character.

The magic was: Great research into clothing for the Middle Ages. A beautiful rhythm to many sentences. Strong overall pace. Some poetic turns of phrase, especially in dialogue. Some wise appraisals of the character of politicians back then that still apply today. And, most important of all, I was often transported back in time.

A followup exercise involving magic's close cousin, alchemy, could be: "Turn the rocks into gold." It would involve going back and replacing the cliches with fresh descriptions. It is hard as hell, because lightning and thunder have been described for thousands of years, but nobody said making magic would always be easy!

Tell the truth.

The world is full of amazing things that happen—that, unbelievably, happen. My own life is full of these things. I am obsessed with the magic that real life lays out for all of us. Most of the time it's so crazy I have no need to make up anything. I just have to tell what I see and hear and smell and taste and feel and sense. You may find it hard to believe.

Folks ask me, about *Ecology*, "How much did you dramatize?" They ask because some of the stories seem more fictional than nonfictional. For some of the stories, such as the day my parents eloped, I was not present to actually know what transpired, so some readers are hesitant to believe the stories.

"In all the stories in which I was an eyewitness," I say, "the stories are as true to fact and tone as possible. In the rest, I told the stories *as they were told to me*, as a sort of omniscient narrator. I made nothing up. I don't know how much they are dramatized, although I did corroborate and incorporate versions of stories from different kinspeople. Everything I said that happened is *probably what happened*."

I should add that in rare and minor cases I fabricate details. Maybe I say the curtains are yellow or the tractor was a John Deere, when in fact I am not certain. Any detail that is fictionalized in my nonfiction is one impertinent to the story but essential for setting a scene. These constructed details may not be truth but in every case were *likely* or *possibly* accurate.

Live in the layers.

When Philip Gerard defined the fourth genre in his seminal book, *Creative Nonfiction: Researching and Crafting Stories from Real Life*, he said that it contains two layers. One is an apparent subject and the other is a deeper subject. This can be thought of as text and subtext or even point and counterpoint.

The apparent subject of Charles Frazier's *Varina*, for example, is a biography of Jefferson Davis's wife. The deeper subject, or subtext, is an attempt to understand how a relatively small percentage of owning class folks persuaded the whole of the South to cling to slavery, at great expense and when an imminent war could not be won. These elite were both slaveholding southerners as well as northerners who benefitted from the work of enslaved people. The text is Varina, the subtext is the tragedy of slavery.

Judy Blunt's essay "Breaking Clean" likewise operates on these two levels. It is apparently and textually about leaving a constrictive life as a ranch wife in eastern Montana. More deeply and subtextually, it's about self-actualization.

Alice Walker's *The Color Purple* is about an African-American girl who is writing letters to god about her rural, isolated life. More deeply, it breaks silence about domestic and sexual violence.

In most any novel we can find two main currents that braid together into a narrative.

When Gerard suggested two layers, I believe that he was thinking of creative nonfiction as opposed to journalism. Journalism has one layer, the text.

Rather than two layers, however, the best nonfiction contains manifold layers.

Terry Tempest Williams's *Refuge* is a great example. It is about breast cancer that occurs in the women in her family and about nuclear testing in the desert. It's also about 1) the landscape of Utah, 2) family, 3) the Mormon religion, 4) birds, and 5) the Great Salt Lake. Multiple layers, if tightly controlled, add depth and richness.

As Stanley Kunitz wrote in his wonderful poem, "The Layers"—

"Live in the layers,
    not in the litter."

Layers in a work, however, have to be pertinent to its driving line. When a writer starts talking about chasing rabbits, well, she is chasing rabbits.

Once a student turned in to me an essay that proved her ability to render a scene. She had an artist's eye and was quick to notice the way a shadow fell. In the wideness of this essay she pulled up myriad memories from childhood to adulthood, from dogs to her mom to superstores to adult care facilities to gardens to art to basketball to ponies. Often there was no link between dogs and nursing homes or her mom and art. It was all too much.

Layering is fine if the reader knows what the text is and what the subtext is, and if each layer helps drive the narrative forward.

To repair an essay with too many layers, clarify the driving line and remove some of the minor, least relevant themes. To repair an essay with only one or two layers, deepen your thinking and do some braiding.

Exercise

Start a page in your journal and begin to list your obsessions. Write as many as you can. Be as abstract as you like (democracy or spoken word or honesty) or as real and particular as you like (your lover's lips or tupelo honey or the color indigo). Keep listing.

Prompt

Pick one item on your list of obsessions and do a four-minute flow-write about it.

16

VOICE

I wanted to be a writer badly. When I was young I read everything I could find about becoming one.

Every how-to told me I needed to "find my voice."

That advice kept me lost for a long time, looking for something but not knowing what I searched for. Finally I figured it out.

"Voice" in writing is not something that can be found—it can only be earned. That is a heretical statement, so please note it and note where you read it. You heard it from me.

Voice is facility with language. Period. Voice is getting comfortable enough with language—in our case this crippled, crazily structured, often inadequate, and sometimes soaring set of hieroglyphics that we call "English"—that who you are and what you believe and what you know comes winging through. Your writing has your stamp on it.

A voice is not a style. Voice is the ability to write complex and interesting sentences using a divergency of structures. Voice is the innate ability to be logical in one's writing. Voice is comfort with the language in which you're writing.

A voice is not given and yet voice is not elusive. I say again, *Voice is earned*. Voice comes to the hard worker, just as luck comes to the brave. Facility is earned through practice, meaning reading and writing and editing.

To find your voice, then, read and write and edit.

When I am asked to judge a contest, I often start by reading the first line of every entry. Then I go back and read each first paragraph. Then I'll read the entries. Nine times out of ten, I know from the first line who is going to win the contest. That's because voice will shine through right away, evident in the ease and facility and beauty of even the first sentence.

That's not always the case. But it's often the case.

Once when I was teaching at a university in my region, I met a young writer from my hometown. That thrilled me immensely—my little hometown had produced another writer! His stories were crazily good, throbbing with energy, but something was off. I figured it out. Here's my note to him:

I think what you need is lots of experience writing. I don't think your voice is developed yet. Having a voice means simply having a familiarity with words, so that you say what needs to be said without effort. Voice is practice. I'd like to have a conversation with you about how much time you actually spend writing—not simply writing for practice, in journals, but writing for others to read. My honest feeling, my friend, is that you haven't even begun to touch the depths of your creativity and ability.

My message to *you*, then: To find your voice, do a lot more writing, a lot more tinkering, a lot more reading. Write until sentences come easy.

Master mechanics

One cannot earn a voice and become a great writer without mastering mechanics. Problems of voice are often problems of mechanics. Call me a fuddy-duddy if you wish, but I suggest that, right now, you add a stylebook to your reading list if you haven't already. I highly recommend *The Elements of Style*, no matter what Buhner said. Strunk and White's classic is a biblical book jam-packed with basic but potent, providential information, when to use a comma or not, when to put a quotation mark inside the end punctuation. When I taught at university I required all my students to buy *The Elements of Style*.

You'll have to force yourself to stay awake and at attention while reading this jewel of a book.

When you open it you have walked into a well-organized workroom where screwdrivers are hanging in order on a pegboard and hammers are lined up by utility. A writer who does not understand mechanics is like a woodworker who doesn't know how to use a planer. You need tools. You watch how craftspeople use the tools. You need to get really good at knowing how these tools work. You learn the rules. You need material. You learn how to judge the material: this is oak and it's going to be harder than pine.

When you write, then, bookmark a style website or keep a stylebook handy. One of the more in-depth and often-used stylebooks is the *Chicago Manual of Style*. There are others. Choose one and stick with a particular style. Your publisher, when she shows up, may use a different style. You, however, will not be judged for dissimilarity but for inconsistency and inaccuracy. The more you adhere to consistency and accuracy, the more apt you are to be published, since the easier your editor's job will be.

Commas in particular

I hate to say this, but I've seen many instances of writers never learning some simple theory of mechanics that should have been learned in elementary school. For some reason many writers wrestle with commas. People don't understand where to place them. If commas are your weakness, study hard. A comma is a pause, a breath. Practice reading aloud a literary book, pausing at each comma.

Commas come with a set of rules that offer a lot of leeway, and the rules keep changing. The Oxford comma is in, the Oxford comma is out. Read and reread Strunk and White's section on commas, which offers the basics.

Other tools

Look up numerals too. Very specific rules mandate when to use numerals and when to write out the words: Eight or 8. Numbers over 10 (or 100, depending on the style) should be in numeral form, with certain exceptions. Unfortunately, you need to know the exceptions.

While you're in the tool shop, look up quotation marks.

The reason for style is that it makes life easier for the reader, and above all else we want the reader to be happy. If the reader isn't happy, nobody's happy. An unhappy reader is going to walk away.

Another reason for style is to help you develop your voice.

I learned with my first book that grammar is many times more complicated than even *The Elements of Style* proposes. I was shocked to work with a professional copyeditor whose edits were far beyond my ken, into the predicate and subjunctive and other esoteric and arcane regulations. Leave the obscurities to the pros if you like, but be functional with the basics.

Rules change

Of course, the basics change. I learned, for example, that when using multiple pronouns as direct objects, to say, "The throng surged toward Silas and me." (I am reminded to use "me" by removing "Silas and," the sentence becoming "The throng surged toward me.") Lately, however, even on National Public Radio, I hear educated commentators saying, "The throng surged toward Silas and I." This makes me crazy, as it does other language police, including Lynne Truss, author of a fun book on grammar, *Eats, Shoots & Leaves: The Zero Tolerance Approach to Punctuation*. I assume that the rules are changing. They always do.

They vary from publisher to publisher as well.

Because of the fluidity of language, a time may come when you get to invent your own styles. You will get to decide if you are going to capitalize Earth the way we capitalize Mars. Make your decisions and stick with a plan and don't look back, like robbing a bank. Get in, get out, nobody gets hurt. Nobody gets caught.

Mostly they'll catch you. A press or a magazine will have its own internal style, and you can fight back or get smarmy, but in the end you'll change the point in question like the rest of us. When the day arrives that you sneak your own style past a pro, then you can mix a highball and rejoice.

Use accurate words

Another mistake is inaccurate use of language, which distills into sloppy writing. Consider this line, straight from a student essay: "She wanted to name me Jada, like the color of her eyes." At first read the sentence looks fine. A reader's eyes will move past the period, into the next sentence, because the reader is looking first for meaning and understands well what this line communicates.

At that line, for me, the boat of the story sprang a tiny leak and began to sink. The color of the mother's eyes is *jada*? *Jada* suggests *jade*. *Jada* is not *jade*. This sentence is easily repaired with the addition of one word. "She wanted to name me Jada, suggesting the color of her eyes."

Consider this sentence: "Her voice rang out in a growl." Honestly, as an officer of writing law, I could not issue a ticket for this sentence because it is not incorrect. It could be defended as poetic. I'm here to tell you that sentence is not poetic. This is an inaccurate use of language, whether in prose or poetry. A growl does not ring out. This sentence tells me that its author has not practiced enough.

We all start out writing like this. I still do it. Hopefully I'm better at catching myself.

If expectations are high, your work is better. Go through your drafts sentence by sentence, and make sure each sentence makes sense, and that it is as structurally sound and as artistic as possible.

The basis of good writing is accuracy in language and in punctuation. That is style. Until that is achieved, art is not possible.

As a writer writes and begins to develop her voice—the ease and facility and beauty of her language—perhaps something else begins to build in her work. It's a kind of energy, a power. Once, at the Feminist Women's Writers Workshop many years ago, on a glacial lake near Ithaca, New York, where as a student I spent a few days with the poet Lucille Clifton, I heard poet Rachel deVries say that a person could hover her hand above a manuscript and feel its power. What deVries suggested was a palpable magic, that powerful words emanate a force and that this energy can be felt. I think of reiki, the bodywork that wrangles energy, unblocking the energetic chakras of a person. Surely if you work hard enough, bolts of energy will fling from your work. It will be hot to the hands. It will spontaneously combust. It will be work that must be hosed down in order to be read.

Exercise

Go find your stylebook and place it on your desk. If you don't have one, subscribe to one online. Look up one thing, which words get capitalized in titles. You'll be surprised.

Prompt

The rule I hate most is...

17

MEANING

Most people don't read creative nonfiction to be entertained. They read it for meaning. They want to understand their own lives. They want to learn. They want to be comforted. They want to be inspired, to hold out hope.

Meaning, actual or implied, makes the difference between adequate writing and great writing. And meaning has to be figured out. By the writer.

A literary nonfiction writer's first job is to "know thyself," a deceptively simple state of consciousness that many people never attain. Knowing thyself will make knowing the world much easier.

Secondly, the writer must be able to recognize the emotion of an event or series of events and use it to his or her advantage, not beating the reader over the head with the emotion—never even mentioning the emotion, perhaps—but understanding it and circling around it and brushing against it. We come to meaning through emotion.

Why it matters

When trying to illuminate the meaning of a story, or a scene, or an event, I sit down with my journal and give myself a few minutes. I attempt to answer the question: *What does this mean to me?*

I ask myself question after question, mining deeper and deeper. *Why am I obsessed with this? What have I learned from it? What will it mean to someone else? What about the event do I want readers to understand? What in one sentence am I trying to tell them?*

Finally I'll find some nugget of gold that makes sense.

Another trick is to ask myself where I think I can publish the piece. *Who will be the audience?* Pondering that is a great way to understand the dangers of having no meaning. Although you may not want to limit yourself to a particular audience, you will.

While we're on the subject of audience, let me say that to write for an audience that is a mother, or a husband, or a good friend, is easy. Those people are charmed by what we write. But an audience that is not my mother has to be convinced. It has to be moved, to tears if possible.

Sometimes my writers balk at my insistence on meaning and tell me, "I intend this to be humor."

I say, Strive for meaning even in your light-hearted pieces. I say, Meaning leads to greatness. I say, Plenty of places publish lighter writing, maybe even more places than for literary work, but the job of a story is to transform, and if there is no meaning, change can not occur.

You never have to actually corral meaning into an essay, but it should always crouch in the back of your mind as you write.

Emotion

I want to say a couple more things about emotion's role in meaning-making. Facts and statistics don't change people. Emotions do. Kittredge said that to me. "Nobody changes their conduct because of ideas, but because of emotions" were the words I wrote in my mini-notebook. But how to create emotion using 26 tiny symbols printed in multitudinous combinations on a flat white sheet of paper?

Robert Olen Butler and Janet Burroway's writing manual, *From Where You Dream*, contains fabulous information about crafting emotion. It's in the chapter "Boot Camp." They say that emotions reside in the senses, and senses originate in the body.

Butler and Burroway work through five ways in which emotions are experienced and thus utilized in writing. Again, I am taking liberty with their list.

1. A sensual reaction inside the body, invisible to others. Your heart speeds up, a muscle begins to tic in your throat.

2. A sensual response that sends signals outside the body, visible to others—gestures, body language, facial expressions, face-flushing, tone of voice. You cross your arms, you lift one eyebrow. These can be observed.

3. Flashes of the past, or as they say, "little vivid bursts of waking dreams." This is in the form of an image.

4. Flashes of the future, what you suspect or know to be coming at you. Also in the form of an image.

5. "At any given moment we, and therefore our characters, are surrounded by hundreds and hundreds of sensual cues," Butler and Burroway wrote. But only a small fraction impinge on our consciousness. Our emotions are what select the sensual cues that we notice. This is not actually a way we experience emotion. It's our response to emotional stimuli—we pick and choose. Although it's not a technique for showing emotion,

it's a prerequisite for meaning-making. It happens naturally, subconsciously.

Allow me to add a way we experience emotion, and this should be at the top of the list. We experience and show emotion through describing what is actually happening, as experienced through the five senses.

We experience emotion through the various non-primary senses as well.

The time needed

Kittredge told me that it takes four minutes to produce an emotion in someone. A reader has a stronger emotional response to a *longer* scene. Therefore, when you get to an important event, slow it down.

How to slow a scene

Writers slow a scene down by slowing *themselves* down, paying more attention, noting more details, checking in with their own bodies, moving carefully. Longer sentences slow things down, as do Latinate words, reflection, and elegance, meaning lyricism.

How to speed up a scene

Boom. You hit them when they don't expect it. You strike to the heart. Your own heart has been struck. Your meaning is clear. Shorter sentences. No reflection. Anglo-Saxon words. Narration as opposed to lyricism.

∼

Exercise

Write an anecdote. When you are done, go back and make sure it contains at least one example of all four ways that Butler and Burroway say that writers show emotion.

～

Prompt

How you broke my heart...

18

BRIDGES

etaphors have to be watched. They're sneaky.
They can turn language into medicine or into
weaponry.

This makes them a powerful tool.

In 2004 Chelsea Green published linguist George Lakoff's
grenade of a book for progressives, *Don't Think of an Elephant.*
Someone says to you, "Whatever you do, *don't think of an
elephant.*" What happens? An elephant is the first thing you
think of. In fact, you have difficulty thinking of anything else.

What we say matters. How we say it matters. People think in
terms of frames and metaphors, which are conceptual structures, meaning a larger credo. One such frame might be that
people deserve jobs. "When the facts don't fit the frames, the
frames are kept and the facts ignored," Lakoff says.

"Who controls the metaphor controls the world," Lakoff
says.

Dr. King

Dr. Martin Luther King, Jr. was a master at metaphor. The Emancipation Proclamation, he wrote, was a "great beacon light of hope" and a "joyous daybreak." "Withering injustice" was like being "seared in the flames." Racial injustice was "quicksand." Segregation was a "desolate valley," racial justice a "sunlit path."

Interestingly, many of Dr. King's metaphors are economic in nature, because the insidious economic oppression of black and brown Americans was a forceful rallying cry. "The Negro lives on a lonely island of poverty in a vast ocean of material prosperity," King wrote. America had written the Negro people *a bad check*. It came back marked *insufficient funds*. America *defaulted* on its *promissory note*.

In the very last speech Dr. King delivered before his heartbreaking murder, he said that he had "been to the mountaintop." He said that he had "seen the promised land." Both of these are metaphors of hope and promise, words that would live forever, a permanent response to an end he seemed to see coming.

Controlling language

Many years ago I was invited to a gathering of nature writers and ecologists in the Cascade Mountains of Oregon. We were meeting to brainstorm more effective metaphors for ecological restoration. The gathering was organized by Kathleen Dean Moore, an environmentalist philosopher and nature writer who understands that humans need the earth to be as ecologically functional as possible. The earth needs humans too. Therefore, humans cannot protect a piece of earth and expect it to take care of itself, nor list a species as threatened and expect it to resurrect on its own. Our metaphorical human hand, which has laid its dark print of loss against all the faces of the planet, needs to fix things. Faced as we are with the necessity of human action, we must breach and blow up and remove and replant. That's restoration.

Moore wondered how writers could talk about restoration so that more people understood the concept, so that it fit their frames, so that the idea of ecological restoration didn't bounce off. How could writers optimize the destiny of wildness?

Medical metaphors

Most metaphors for ecological restoration have been medical in nature, Moore said. A forest is *healing*, it is *recovering*, it is *renewing* itself. Ecologists have a *prescription* for restoring a forest's health. We watch its *rebirth*.

But a cutover pine flatwoods is not sick.

Once, an ecologist asked a woman what she thought of a certain prescribed burn. The woman, a nurse, had worked in the burn unit of a hospital for years and years. "It just sickens me," she said.

Here are more bad metaphors that I collected at the gathering: I don't know how to *manage a forest* but I can *mow a lawn*. I don't know how to *fix a river* but I can *plumb a toilet*. The best kind of forest is a *working* forest.

"If these old metaphors aren't working, what metaphors might?" asked Moore. She assembled the participants into small groups and tasked each group with inventing a new metaphor for environmental restoration.

Re-creation? Since the primeval world was creation, is restoration *re-creation*, us humans assisting as lesser gods in a new creation?

A tapestry? Is creation a tapestry, woven by millions of years of evolution, and we the re-weavers or the darners?

An orchestra? Is restoration a kind of orchestra, a concert of returning species? Or might it be a less structured arrangement, maybe a jazz ensemble or jam session or sing-along, each species of animal and plant filling a frequency? Could we, like the Australian aborigines, live among songlines, singing restored places into being?

After hours of discussion, colleagues in my group decided to liken restoration to courtship, marriage, and home-making.

Marriage has no destination in mind, but is a process—as is restoration. Home is a place of intimacy, sustenance, sanctuary, return—as is a wild place. A home houses a family of beings tied to each other, supported by community—as with an ecosystem. Further, we would never presume simply to *manage* our family or home. Therefore, love should be included in the "management" of a forest.

We framed a marriage vow: *Let's see what we can do to joyfully create an enduring home together, for the rest of our lives and our children's lives.*

Environmental thinker Joanna Macy describes the "world as lover" in her book *World as Lover, World as Self.* Macy writes, "Trees, rocks, and plants surrounded us with a living presence as intimate and pulsing as our own bodies."

Metaphors as weapons

After I returned home I began to think about language in a less innocent way. Lakoff talks about the ingenious use of metaphor by politicians, especially conservative ones. *No Child Left Behind* meant the opposite—as children couldn't pass standardized tests, they were often passed along without knowing basic academic skills like how to read or how to multiply. The children weren't left behind but their academic skills were.

The *Healthy Forests* Initiative proposed clearcutting. Health as surgery. Remove the tumor. Remove even the breast that is without tumor, to prevent it becoming diseased. Remove the forest that can burn.

The two well-used words *Clean Coal* hide an entire backstory. We know coal to be black, but if it's clean, then it's black like obsidian, and washable. You can take a polishing rag to it. If it's clean, nobody gets hurt.

In actuality, nothing about coal is clean. It is dirty start to finish—coal miners get black lung, babies get asthma, air gets polluted, and streams get contaminated with coal ash, which contains high levels of heavy metals.

Listening for metaphors

When the U.S. stock markets fell in late 2007, the language used in the media was gripping. *The economy is in freefall. Markets are tanking. We are in a meltdown. Executives are given golden parachutes. They should be given a haircut.*

One newscast compared the economy to the movie *Titanic.* Most of us were going to die.

On guns

After Congresswoman Gabrielle Giffords was shot in 2011, Dr. Mary Hamer wrote about how common gun metaphors are in our society: *in the crosshairs, pistol whip, easy mark, fired up, halfcocked, bang for the buck, bite the bullet.* She advocated for a language of peace and respect instead of a language of war. Yes, "free speech is an important right of citizens," Hamer wrote, "but free speech also implies responsible speech." She wrote, "Words are powerful. May we all choose and use our words wisely."

Climate crisis

I paid attention to the metaphors as climate scientists rang their alarm bells about global warming more and more loudly.

We humans were playing Russian roulette with our future. A firehose of information was coming at us. The gun was pointed at our grandchildren. We were also setting records almost daily. (Record-setting sounds like a good thing.)

Even the phrase *global warming* was wrong. Folks in northern Ontario might want to live in a place more like Florida. *Climate change* was wrong too, since change can be good.

I stopped saying *global warming* or even *climate change*. Like many others, I started to call the problem climate *crisis* or climate *disruption* or climate *destabilization*. Scientists predicted an increase in violent storms, the melting of ice-caps and glaciers and permafrost, a rise in sea-levels, a skewing of seasons, and yes, a rise in global temperatures. *Crisis* is not good.

Awakening to the power of metaphor is essential to a writer, especially one with a mission.

❦

Exercise

Add metaphors and similes to your work as you think of them.

❦

Prompt

Do flow-writes to think of metaphors. "This reminds me of a _____." and "When I think of this, I think of a _____."

19

THE OTHER SIDE

Most people have an idea for a book and they want to write a book, but they never actually get started. The same is true of an essay. The idea of writing is far more appealing and enjoyable than the experience of doing it.

The hardest thing in the world is generation—a writer has to produce the stories. That means you have to nail your shoes to the floor beneath your writing desk. Your friends and family want you to watch movies, visit places, hike trails, bake cakes, make love. The last thing you want to do is sequester yourself in your writing cubby. But you have to.

Show up

You'll never get anywhere unless you show up, and showing up is not easy. In fact, it's about the hardest thing you'll ever do. Most people can't do it. Much of the time I can't.

Finish

Then, you have to finish. "People write promising pieces but never finish them," Kittredge said.

A writer is always in the middle of a long and painful process. By the time she gets to revisions she has done the hardest part of all, the part that most people never actually accomplish, and that is getting the rough draft on paper. Write through once.

Consider this note I wrote to one of my students:

> In these beginning pages I find wonderful moments, great sentences, and interesting introspection. You have a wonderful start here. As time goes on you'll have a beautifully strong and fluid voice from which to tell your story. I don't want any of my suggestions to hamper you from moving forward valiantly and capably and quickly. So if this were me, I would not pause in my writing to do any tinkering or revising. What you need more than anything right now is to get the entire story onto paper.

When I edit a piece that I did not write, I first appreciate that the writer stuck with the project to the end. She did the work. She put the final period on the final sentence of the final page. That's huge. Congratulations are in order. After I acknowledge that amazing accomplishment, I can tackle what's going well and then what's wrong.

Get to the end

My advice to everybody is, *Keep going. Write. Write and do not waste time. Get to the end.* Afterwards you can begin the process of winnowing, patching, deleting, sanding, ordering, replacing, and otherwise making yours the powerful story it can be.

Exercise

Set a time to show up at your desk and work on a longer project. Start with a small amount of time, even five minutes. I would do this every day. Stick to your promise to yourself. Show up.

Prompt

What scares me the most...

20

HIGHER GROUND

M ost people never realize an important fact: the finest sorcery in writing happens during revising. Revising is absolute joy. Almost everybody needs an editor, and the first one you employ should be yourself.

My writing process is to get on paper a rough draft—cruel, crude, and unlovely.

Then I wait, a couple of weeks, longer if possible. The longer the wait the better the revision, up to a certain point. The secret is to let enough time pass that you forget the work before you come back. A writer with a good memory is in trouble. If your memory is poor, like mine, you're in luck. A year is too long to wait.

Then I crawl through the manuscript on hands and knees.

I wait another while and walk through again. I repeat this until the piece improves enough to imagine presenting it to the world. It's a tedious procedure. However, each time I pass through a text I see problems and possibilities, poetic leaps of thought, metaphors I had not considered, entire structural flaws. The more traverses I make, the better the piece becomes.

Small changes often make large impacts, which is why

revising is so powerful. The change of one word can affect a paragraph or page or even the entire piece.

The steps

First get the story line—the structure—functional and captivating. Next concentrate on polishing sentences one by one. Keep tinkering, shaping, and burnishing. Sit with the work in the evenings. Or in the mornings. Then get a reader you trust to read the whole thing. Then another. Share it with a writing group if you have one.

Don't send this out yet.

Writers get disillusioned by the time required to revise, and I often find myself saying, *Don't give up. You can find a publisher for this if you go farther with it.*

The more buffing, the more readers you'll have and the better a book, or essay, or whatever you're working on, will sell.

As good as you can

Many years ago at a conference I introduced myself to the gifted editor and poet Barbara Ras, who then worked at Sierra Club Books. I described a project I was working on. "When you get it as good as you can," she said. "Send it to me." That line was very helpful. It meant I had a limit. I could only get a book as good as I could get it. Afterwards, I'd need someone else to get it to a higher plane.

Hopefully, after you have got your project as good as you can, a stellar editor will emerge. Most people underestimate the value of editors and get all puffed up about someone messing with their baby. Please believe me when I say that great editors are hard to find, increasingly uncommon, and essential to the writing process. An editor is a writer's bestie. Truly. Everything I am was made possible because I've had some fabulous, discerning, and utterly relentless editors. Without Emilie Buchwald at Milkweed my book *Ecology* would have been a nice package of fire starter.

When an editor appears, pray she's brilliant, and pray that you are emotionally free enough from your ego to take her comments and use them to make a bestseller or at least a book to be remembered through the ages, even if it doesn't make the charts.

Often I find with young writers that the first page of a manuscript is the worst, and the pages consistently gain clarity. Overwriting at the beginning is common, understandable, and almost unavoidable, because to enter a new story, down one path, is a struggle for anyone. Over time, if you're lucky, and I hope you are, a story becomes more and more clear and interesting.

Occasionally the opposite happens, that a story starts strong and wanes.

Revising is hard work, no doubt, but the more stories you push through and make functional, the easier the next revision becomes.

Mistakes obscure

A few years ago a friend sent me a manuscript that I loved, a really wonderful, esoteric, filled-with-understated-passion, burgeoning piece that grabbed me. I thought he had a marvelous first draft, and I was excited about seeing it published. But it was filled with grammatical errors, and when there are problems with tidiness, addressing the deeper, more problematic issues is hard. I made marks all over my friend's draft. My humble advice (and request) was for him to revise it, going through fastidiously, line by line, and then send it to me again, perhaps double-spaced, so that I could focus on artistry.

As far as I know, my friend never returned to that piece of

work. My belief is that he hit his inner glass ceiling, a concept from Gay Hendricks' *The Big Leap* that means limiting inner beliefs, mindsets, usually from childhood, that hold a person back. My friend realized that I saw genius, and he was not kind enough to himself to honor his genius. Most of us are not used to thinking of ourselves as holy people, as magicians, as world healers. We can be incredibly unkind to ourselves. Rather than doing the (very) hard work of learning to love ourselves, we'd rather ignore the person who points out our genius.

Oh well. More room on the bookstore shelves for me.

Occasionally I'm sent a manuscript for whatever reason—to blurb, to look at—and I return it. I can be blunt. "I'm not able to write you a blurb," I'll say. "I think you can have a book in here, but you're not finished. Meanwhile, I have marked up your manuscript with some thoughts and ideas. I hope at least some of these will help you create a fine book."

This is important. You only get one first chance with the great story of your life, and there's no reason to blow it and every reason to make it as good and writerly as you can make it. Every bad piece you publish will make your next one harder to place. Or should.

Get it right

The first thing to revise for is accuracy, since most of us don't want blatant errors in our prose. Then revise for voice and style, moving closer to the words that best fit, to the sentence construction that resonates. I revise for other elements as well:

1. To show not tell
2. To make sure I've described characters
3. To include certain elements, such as a sense of place.

In workshops, I'll often have writers take a half hour to write a scene. I follow that exercise with specific and quick revisions such as *Add a color*. I do this mainly to give writers an idea of how little genius comes through divine intervention and how much comes through perspiration, since each revision brings the writer closer to essence and singularity.

HERE ARE general thoughts on revising.

Re-read.

Re-read everything before showing it to anyone, at the very least. I know, you've heard it a hundred times. I'm saying it to myself as much as to you. If I'm on deadline I don't want to do it either. But ya gotta.

Read aloud.

When you read a piece out loud you are able to catch many more problems than if you read it silently.

Correct any shoddiness, large or small.

Simplify your work.

Go through your draft with an eye toward cutting any unnecessary word, phrase, or sentence. Slash any repetition or any obvious idea. Anything that makes the reader feel dumb should vanish.

Cut relentlessly. If something's not relevant, hack it out.

Many years after I left Missoula I returned as a visiting

writer to the university. As we workshopped a paper, one of my students said of another's work, "How clean and simple the language is." That comment is gold.

Look at this passage from E.B. White in *One Man's Meat:* "It struck me as we worked our way homeward up the rough bay with our catch of lobsters and a fresh breeze in our teeth that this was what the fight was all about. This was it. Either we would continue to have it or we wouldn't, this right to speak our own minds, haul our own traps, mind our own business, and wallow in the wide, wide sea."

How clean and simple the language is.

Study this quote from A. Wainwright in *A Pennine Journey: The Story of a Long Walk in 1938.* "I love these lonely hills of Lakeland with a love that is beyond comprehension. I could not attempt to write of the quiet joy that long days in their company have brought to me...They were calling me; their voice was the moaning of the wind amid the rocks of chasm and precipice, the rush of cataract and murmur of mountain stream...There are no hills like the hills of Lakeland."

How elegant the writing, how clean and simple.

A pulse is beating in each of those passages.

Have you read Per Pettersen? Willa Cather? Kent Haruf? Ernest Gaines? Larry Brown? Read his *Joe*—that simplicity is divine. Read Cormac McCarthy's *All the Pretty Horses*.

Eliminate filler.

I sometimes advise writers to do a computer search for any word that keeps popping up in a text. AI would be great for this. I recommended that one young woman search for the number of times she used the word "still," as in "I still liked him." I knew she was going to fall out of her chair. "Still" is bad because it's usually filler.

I had her search for the word "hurt" as well. "Hurt" is bad because it's telling, not showing.

In almost every case, the word "just" is useless filler. Search for and delete it when appropriate. "Just" just drains the blood from your sentences.

Much of language usage is subconscious. We surprise ourselves with our behaviors.

Cut a lot.

I'm going to say it again. Scout your piece looking for any possible words, phrase, sentence, or paragraph that can be cut. Trim anything that is not powerful, real, and meaningful. If a word is not useful, if it doesn't serve a purpose, it doesn't need to be there. A simple, spare text is most powerful. Repetition and superfluity, even implied, drags down writing like a virus.

As Kittredge told me, "Cut to where if you deleted one more sentence the story wouldn't be understandable." Poet Richard Hugo said, "A poem is never finished until you have to cut your favorite line." Yikes.

Work on the level of the sentence.

I divide writing into seven levels, and deciding which level is most important has kept me happily occupied on long walks.

- the word
- the sentence
- the paragraph
- the section
- the essay or chapter
- the book
- the body of work.

I've come to believe that of all levels, the sentence is most pivotal, and to improve your sentences, I suggest to study the sentences of great writers, copying out beautiful passages you discover. Most of us—and I'm guilty first—don't ever approach the wild possibilities of sentence structure. Faulkner's sentences will, of course, humble anyone.

Avoid fragments and run-ons. Or not.

In general, successful writers prove their prowess with engaging, interesting, and complete sentences, and readers who've been reading world literature for years expect whole sentences. In this paradigm, fragments are cars stalled on a busy freeway. They impede flow. If a reader gets to page three and encounters a fragment, the reader reads this fragment as a mistake. In an entire piece, three or four fragments will cause a massive pile-up. If the reader has to brake to a stop and re-read a confusing line, that is an accident waiting to happen.

However, fragments aren't incorrect. The trick is how to use them. They require literary maturity and logic.

The writer of sentence fragments would be wise to establish from the very first that they will be using fragments. Throw in one right away. Then another.

Most beginners who want to use fragments will do so for a while, and then when the book gets rolling they find themselves writing in complete sentences. They'll toss in a fragment occasionally. In order not to shock the reader with assumptions of idiocy I recommend establishing fragments as part of your style right from the beginning. And following through.

Otherwise, turn fragments into complete sentences and use them throughout.

Use fragments sometimes.

Fragments are exceedingly useful, glorious really, for packing punches. They make lovely surprises. When you need to speed up a passage, they're gasoline. For example, I really love the one-word sentence: "Yet." If I wrote that I'd keep it! I love the fragment "Or not."

Watch how many sentences you begin with a conjunction.

Conjunctions are among the least powerful ways to begin a sentence. And. But. Or. You nail your sentence to a wall right away and it flaps there, trying to fly. Take out the conjunction and reread the sentence and you'll see it reads better. In most cases.

A great sentence leaps off the page at you.

One of my students wrote, *There is a moment before movement, a step before the step, a tiny gap between thought and action. In the heartbeat between deciding on a course and actually taking it, there is a breath of air.*

That is beautiful. That is the real work, right there.

Another wrote this striking line: *Autumn is running behind this year so the grass is still green, and even in weak light the baby peach trees look like campfires.* What can you not love about this sentence? Again, I wish it were mine.

Another wrote, *I have always loved the sound of money hitting the bottom of a jar.*

Wow, is what I say.

Vary sentence length.

Once I was invited to give a convocation at Rabun Gap School in the mountains of northern Georgia. Students had been asked to read my first book and write their own personal narratives. Teacher Woody Malot sent me a handout he'd given to the students, a list of ways to revise. One involved sentence length. "Try mixing compound, complex, simple, and interrogative sentences, and try inverting the basic subject-verb order."

There you have it. That's a start.

Work at the level of the word.

In my mind the level of the word ties for first place with the level of the sentence in what's most important in writing.

- Study words, collect them, admire them, employ them.
- Find where you've used the same word twice and change one of them.
- Change one passive or linking verb to an action verb.
- Change one Latinate word to an Anglo-Saxon one.
- Add a random word you really love.

Revive the sensual, starting with the eyes.

Add a color. If you already have a color, add another. Leon Stokesbury at a workshop I attended had students, after writing a poem, add a color that also served as a noun. "Persimmon" was his example, as in "the persimmon dress." Other colors that stand as nouns: Lime. Hazel. Salmon. Coral. Ruby. Ivory. Violet. Indigo. Olive. Emerald.

Add a shape.

Describe folks. Add a word or phrase or line of description. The reader can't see a person you're talking about unless you tell us how they look. And don't pile all the description up in one place. Spread it out.

Add an odor.

Add a sound.

Can you get in a taste?

What about something palpable?

How does something feel to the fingers? Include a texture.

Give readers information they need.

I knew a writer who tended to refer to things a reader could not understand, like diving from cliffs into unknown rivers or family members who raised some kind of plant medicine or an unnamed place where an ancestor had died. These references would get a single mention.

A reader needs info. Who dove? What cliffs? What rivers? Where? What family members? What medicine? Who was there? Were you there? How was that for you?

More importantly, Why? Why? Why?

A writer is in trouble if a reader is beset with questions for which the answers are not forthcoming. You keep a reader guessing too long, you run the risk of losing them. Mystery is beguiling but it can also be mean—a withholding, a bad kind of control, a dementia.

A few paragraphs into the piece someone casually says, "Our family reunions are always held here," and the reader thinks, "Oh, this is a family reunion. It's held at this park." Tell us outright that you are at a family reunion, at a little county park that has been special for your family and that was special to native Americans as a dance ring. You can't keep a reader guessing too long about what is happening. You'll look up and they'll be gone.

Remember, we readers are blind and cannot see anything unless you show us.

Place the reader.

Sometimes I am pages into reading a story before I learn that it takes place in Wisconsin. I feel disoriented, then a little angry. My advice is to show readers where we are and what decade we're in and what is there. Withholding temporal and geographical information will cripple you. (This is different from withholding information in order to build tension.)

Once I wrote an essay about a mule who lives on our farm. At a weekend workshop that explored sense of place, I gave a reading and presented this essay. To my dismay I realized that the mule story could have happened anywhere. It contained no particularities that showed where it happened.

Well, it's a universal story, one could say.

But it wasn't universal. It happened on my farm, in the south of Georgia, in the southern coastal plains, a place with a history and intimacy with mules. Very little in the essay illuminated the particulars of my locale. I challenged myself to revise, adding in lines of description and scene to reveal place.

On the other hand, trust the reader.

Don't tell a reader too much. Expect genius. Assume you're writing for a person who's well-educated, a reader of *Harper's*, for example. Write as if Bill McKibben were going to read your work, and you don't want to piss him off by writing as if he only finished grade school.

Of course the more-sage advice is to write for your intended audience.

Think about ambiguous or anonymous "it."

As a pronoun, "it" modifies the last preceding noun. In our colloquial, spoken language, we use "it" very loosely, as in "It looks like the car is stolen."

"It looks." *What* exactly is looking?

"It's raining." What is raining? The day is raining? The cloud is raining?

"It's sunny." The sun is sunny?

Or in hundreds of other ways.

Consider this sentence I lifted from the essay of a student:

He liked to talk, but he was also very quiet, quiet in his head, so that when words did come out, it seemed inconvenient.

Words seemed inconvenient? Talk? His head?

If "it" refers to a noun you used at the beginning of a sentence, and you have used another noun since you pumped out the primary one, make sure "it" refers to the noun you intend. A student wrote, *In dancing, the leader leads and the follower follows. You have to surrender to this fundamental agreement or it doesn't work.* My guess is that the "it" does not refer to the agreement but to the dance.

Seek a clarity of language. Search your texts for "it" and try, try, try to make sure that "it" modifies something. Ask yourself what "it" represents. If you can't figure out an answer, rewrite the sentence. Of course you're allowed to say "It's raining," but your writing should not be crawling with wayward "it." Understand what each represents and use it correctly.

I know I'm being persnickety here and I should apologize for it. But I won't. Precision is important because we writers are trying to further our civilization. Help us.

Avoid passive voice, if possible.

The first lake trout was netted, wrote one of my students.

No. Somebody did something here. A real somebody netted a real damned trout.

Go through your manuscript and work on action. Change passive to active, remembering that *there is* and *there are* are passive voice. Of course, just to cover my butt let me say there are instances, few and far between, where passive is best.

Balance syntax.

I didn't know a thing about syntactic balance until I went to graduate school. What the term means is that words and phrases should be balanced grammatically, especially around punctuation. What occurs on one side of a conjunction, for example, should balance syntactically with what occurs on the other.

Look at this sentence I stole from a student paper, *I wore a swingy black dress, black flats, and my blonde hair down.* This writer has used a series, and the first two items in the series are nouns, items of clothing that can be worn. The third item in the series is not something that can be worn, although confusingly we say that we do, and that last item includes an adverb, hair down. The simplest solution is to rewrite it, *I wore a swingy black dress and black flats, with my blonde hair down.* The writer could rewrite with three nouns, *I wore a black dress, black flats, and loose hair.* That sounds weird. *I wore a black dress, black flats, and a black bow in my hair.* There. You're wearing all black.

Here's another. *She traded oak trees, winding sycamores, and warm weather that baked winter blues from your bones, for flat lands and frozen winters.* The first two items in the first series are nouns with adjectives, oak trees and winding sycamores. The third item is a noun with an adjective but also with a descriptive clause dragging behind like toilet paper stuck on a shoe. Think of a balance scale. Its pivot is the comma after "bones." In one pan of the scale are three nouns and in the other are two. One has two trees and a reference to climate. The second has no trees and a reference to climate.

And tell me, what is a "winding sycamore?" Could she possibly mean a winding road lined with sycamores?

I'm going to rewrite it. *She traded oaks, sycamores, and blistering summers for birches, firs, and long winters.*

Yes, I know that sentence is anal. I am making a point. Are you with me?

Use "a" versus "the" when needed.

I will never forget this rule, which I learned from my most exalted of teachers, Wendell Berry. In the summer of 1995 I attended the Environmental Writing Workshop, sponsored by the University of Montana, which took place at Teller Wildlife Refuge outside Missoula. I often find Iowa-style writing workshops useless, but when I was in my early thirties and wanting to write, hanging with Wendell Berry was titanic. Wendell is a scholar of mechanics. I learned a semester's worth of English grammar from him in a couple of days.

At the beginning of the week, when he would point out gaffes in someone's essay, gratitude that the piece wasn't mine would flood me. When my essay came up in the queue, I had my turn.

Wendell said to use "a" at first mention of a noun. Once the object is identified, a writer can refer to it as "the." *I came to a gate. I opened the gate.*

Who would have known? This is not how we speak. But it's an incredibly smart and helpful rule to know.

Be aware that someone may accuse you of anthropomorphism.

This is the attribution of human characteristics to animals and has, in general, been frowned upon by science. A scientist would not presume to know what a horse or squirrel or even a bonobo thinks.

Anthropomorphism can also apply to anything non-human. Consider this sentence from a student: *He lost his job, but received full retirement, because it was the eighties, I guess, and progress lagged slow and skinned its knees along the marathon.* This says that progress was skinning its knees. I can't imagine progress having knees and definitely not skinning them.

Here's another. *Adrenaline fingered the back of my neck.*

I don't see it. A trickle of liquid hormone tickles the back of her neck? I would revise, *I felt something like fingers on the back of my neck. It had to be adrenaline.* Or, *I felt adrenaline's fingers on the back of my neck.*

Or something like that.

Or not.

Another of my students wrote, *Guilt screeched and scratched at my insides.* Really? Guilt is a wildcat? Trapped inside you?

Let white space do its job.

Without white space, there is no breath. Words have tiny breaths between them, sentences have longer breaths, paragraphs even longer. At the end of a section a reader can draw a breath past the diaphragm and down into the belly.

Please, give the reader time to breathe. White space allows a reader to rest or think for a second. Or it sets up emphasis.

Here is as good a place as any to remind you that short sentences speed up action, long sentences slow action down.

Circle qualifiers.

Qualifiers are words like "maybe" and "perhaps" and "a bit" and "somewhat." These are weak, wishy-washy, bleached-out words that do not denote strength and capability but *qualify* what you are saying and question your credibility.

The cake was *pretty* good. The house was *kind of* spooky. Dave was *probably* right.

Instead of saying, The cake was good. The house was spooky. Dave was right.

Qualifiers magnify indecision and tentativeness, traits you don't want magnified. You want to act and write with power. You want to write powerful things. You want to *be* powerful. Go do it.

Watch repetition, unless it's your style.

Weirdly, repetition is also a poetic element.

I remove references to products and brands.

I do this because I've long been a critic of our economic system, capitalism, which continues to destroy much of what I hold dear. I do not advertise for corporations for free. Not usually.

I stay aware of references to driving and flying.

Also cell phones and other devices. This is my personal schtick. Artists create society. If I'm not walking and feeling the wind pick up, smelling honeycomb on a guy's overalls, hearing an incessant phoebe, I'm not alive, and neither is my character. And I want to live in a world that is alive, embodied, hopeful.

"Revise for strangeness."

I read this mysterious advice from poet Brenda Hillman, and for many years I didn't know what she meant. I'm not going to explain it to you, but simply lay it out for you to ponder. Revise for strangeness.

Said another way, Unpack the weird.

Henry James proclaimed that there are only two emotional states—excitement and lack of excitement. Unfortunately, excitement is more interesting. So get weird.

Don't explode.

Please remember to be careful not to fall into the syndrome that only things that explode are interesting. When I studied with Wendell Berry he pointed out this sentence in my essay: *When the man told me who he worked for, the room exploded.*

"Do you literally mean the room exploded?" Berry asked.

I laughed. "No."

"Well, then," he said, "you need a more accurate verb."

Make people say interesting things.

In real-life dialogue we use a lot of *uh*'s and *okay*'s. Most dialogue is flat, drab, and bland. Creative nonfiction writers need to be true to actual conversations as they happened, but that can cripple a serious literary piece. Spiff up the dialogue, and that, I believe, should be done not by falsifying but by cutting, lots of cutting.

Revise to build tension.

How I published as much as I did early on is a mystery, because I ignored one element crucial to good writing. Tension.

And most writing doesn't have it.

How to write a story that nobody wants to put down? *You have to know what tension is, and you have to learn how to build it into a story.*

I credit Benjamin Percy's *Thrill Me* with opening my eyes. Actually, that book threw a pan of ice-water on me. I'd heard endlessly about tension. But something about the way Percy laid it out woke me up.

People want to know what happens to other people. That's one of the beauties of us humans. Therefore, once people get engaged in an outcome, they will not. stop. reading. until they find out what happens.

Sometimes we writers get lucky, and tension is inherent in a piece. For example, what is more poignant than a farm family threatened by a coal plant?

Flannery O'Connor talks some about this, about the inherent tension in culture, including in the south a set of manners that belies violence: "A great deal of the Southern writer's work is done for him before he begins," she wrote in *Mystery and Manners*. Barry Hannah said something similar to me once as we stood on the banks of Sardis Lake. "You live here in Mississippi, stuff's just handed to you."

Sometimes the tension is handed to you. Mostly you have to create it.

Meting information out in morsels is one way to do it. You gotta become a tease.

Strive for a first line that keeps a person going to the second line, then a first paragraph that grabs the reader and hypnotizes them and seduces them, so that the reader devours the second paragraph. And so on.

Once a friend interviewed me for a piece and then gave me the huge favor of letting me see it before it went to print. She's a fabulous writer, and her first line read:

> Growing up in Baxley, Georgia, writer and environmental advocate Janisse Ray learned early that even when there wasn't much else of value around, stories about the people and places of her "small, sleepy town" held power.

I asked her if she would cut "wasn't much else of value around" because I was surrounded by things of value growing up. And I suggested a way she could build tension.

> Growing up, writer Janisse Ray learned on the front porches of Baxley, Georgia something that would set the course of her life.

That's not the greatest first line in the world, but you see what I'm doing. I'm simplifying the sentence and also teasing you so that you want to keep reading and learn what I learned on the front porches of my hometown.

Okay, go do it. Go back to something you're working on and figure out how you can revise the first line so that you withhold something that we desperately want to find out.

Put characters at cross purposes.

From mystery writer Kathleen George in Pittsburgh I learned the term "cross purposes," which is a three-way relationship in which two of the parties know something the third party does not. This, my dears, will tip your readers to the edges of their chairs. Type out this phrase "cross purposes," and tack it above your desk.

Be careful with facts.

Figure out ways to lace facts and figures into a text seamlessly, in small portions. A whole page of fairly boring history about hunting laws does not encourage people to keep reading. Hopefully, of course, by the time you need to explain these hunting statutes the reader has fallen in love with you as a writer or with your character on the page and is not going anyplace. Still, keeping a reader's patience and tolerance in mind does not hurt the outcome.

Get help.

You are going to need help to make any story sing.

I recommend at least letting another person read a piece before you send it off. You want to make sure that it truly is understandable. You want a fresh reader, since one already familiar with the piece, including yourself, will fill in blanks that a fresh reader can't fill in, if indeed there are blanks.

Friends and colleagues may be able to read sections and give you feedback. If you can join a creative nonfiction writing group, join it. Only trust the people whose sensibilities are similar to yours and whose comments resonate. If you don't have faith in a certain comment, don't use it. If what I say doesn't feel right, ignore it.

What I've learned about myself as a writer is how difficult it is to keep climbing to ever-better places. I'd like to be a great writer and all I know to do is keep asking for help in getting there. Keep studying, keep taking classes, keep reading, and, most of all, keep writing.

Think of something as simple as font.

Here's a practical matter. The font you use for the manuscript cannot be amateurish. Writers are obligated to use a typewriter-like font so that publishers get a general idea of length and bulk of a work. A pretty font shouts out that a beginner is trying to overcome content with presentation. "I want to be more than I am right now." The font on the title page is an immediate and gigantic clue of experience. Please change it to a plain one. Twelve-point text is the norm. Take the date off each page because that is a waste of ink.

Consider epigraphs.

I carefully sought an epigraph for the top of each chapter of the finished draft of my first book. I was lucky enough to have my friend Rick Bass read the manuscript. He axed every epigraph. "Fuck Chekhov," he wrote. "We don't want to hear from Chekhov. We want to hear from you." He meant to quit relying on other people's wisdom—this was the chance and time to impart my own.

If you have found a perfect epigraph, you will not want to trash it. Consider killing most. Epigraphs weaken the narrative. We want your wisdom. Not Ralph Ellison's. Not Robin Kimmerer's. Not Peter Matthiessen's. Not Janisse's.

Crowd-source edits.

Social media taught me that I'm not as smart as I thought. Name *any* subject and someone knows more about it than I do, and that person can be found on social media. It's full of wizards and whiz kids. Folks have incredible interests, passions, obsessions, and specialties. I've found that someone has a smart, beats-Google understanding on every possible subject in the world.

And it's fun. It's real people, engaging with you. You get closer to somebody.

I put this to full advantage as a writer. I often crowd-source ideas and solutions and problems. If I don't know what weed I'm looking at, crowd-source. If I want to know if Mercury is retrograde, ask.

I learned from crowd-sourcing on social media that a bird I'd been seeing was a black-bellied whistling duck. I had looked through every bird book I own, and they all said whistling ducks don't live where I live. Finally I asked online, and in five minutes I had a treasure chest of information. Apparently these ducks have been moving northward and they now live where I live.

I got so enamored with crowd-sourcing research on social media that I extended it to a book. When I independently published *The Woods of Fannin County* I asked readers to please let me know if they spotted an error. I had tried my best to find and fix every single typo or mistake, but for sure:

- Some people know English grammar and rhetoric better than I.
- Some people are better spellers than I.
- Some people know more about every single subject on the earth than I.

In response, folks let me know that:

- Baseball doesn't have a halftime.
- Hemptown Creek doesn't flow to the Atlantic. It flows to the Gulf.
- A woman who has birthed 10 children is not going to have "full, still beautiful" breasts.
- The snakes in the fireplace were first identified as timber rattlers. Later, when Bobby is talking to someone, he calls them cottonmouths.

After a while the edits quit coming, so I figured we had them all. But after a year a biologist found a new one.

Dear Janisse,

I finally got around to reading your book. What an incredible story. I don't see how those kids survived, especially the baby. When you first announced the publication, you asked for readers to let you know of any typos or errors. I have one: On page 110. "...sleet had turned to hail." I always thought hail was associated with summer thunderstorms, not winter storms. I foresee this book becoming a movie. Don't you? Wonderful writing.—S.

Okay, can sleet turn to hail? I went to Google.

USA Today said, "Sleet forms in winter storms, while hail is a warm-season type of precipitation." Crap, I thought, I have to make another change in the book. (When you independently publish via Amazon, in order to make an edit you pull down your book file, make the change, then wait for Amazon to approve the changes. Sometimes this can take a couple of days —time that the book is not actually selling. So I'm never happy about having to make edits.)

I kept researching hail versus sleet.

FOX Weather: "Hail is the one frozen precipitation that *can* fall no matter the date on the calendar or the temperature outside." But who would trust FOX Weather?

National Geographic Society: "Sleet is a type of precipitation distinct from snow, hail, and freezing rain." Okay, maybe sleet is not hail.

NOAA saved me: "Hailstones begin as embryos, which include graupel or sleet, and then grow in size." If we believe NOAA, sleet can turn to hail.

What began as a simple question got more and more complicated as I read, and suddenly there was a new word I'd never heard before, *graupel*, which some sites distinguish as wet and soft while hail is hard and dry.

At some point I closed down the search. I am not going to peruse meteorology journals to fine-tune the science of winter precipitation.

I'm so grateful that this friend pointed out this possible problem. I would never have known all about this.

One possible shortfall is that crowd-sourcing may make you feel vulnerable. Sometimes when we ask questions others scoff at us. You'll notice that I did not crowd-source the question about sleet and hail. That one felt as if I should have known the answer. If you feel vulnerable, don't put yourself at risk. Use private methods of research. Hire an editor.

Usually I don't mind looking like a doofus to the masses because I'm trying to get something I need. When I make a mass inquiry, I filter out the mansplaining and womansplaining (which happens, y'all know). I look for hotshots who're also nice people, which is most of them. Some-body kindly tells me what I need 99 percent of the time, as if my Friends group is an encyclopedia. It's strange. I love it.

That's my pro-tip. Try using your crowd of friends to do your research. Or to edit your work. Or in whatever ways I haven't even considered.

~

Exercise

Go back through a piece you finished recently. Mark all the qualifiers.

~

Prompt

Maybe...

21

GOLDEN STRANDS

I n the 17th century the Japanese poet Basho used a metaphor for writing of following a thing that shines like gold:

> Your poetry issues of its own accord when you
> And the object become one—
> when you have plunged deep enough into the
> object
> to see something like a hidden glimmering
> there.

William Blake wrote in "Jerusalem. The Emanation of a Giant Albion,"

> I give you the end of a golden string
> Only wind it into a ball,
> It will land you in at Heaven's gate
> Built in Jerusalem's wall.

William Stafford talks about the idea of a thread, albeit not a golden one, in his poem, "The Way It Is."

> There's a thread you follow. It goes among
> things that change. But it doesn't change.

Ralph Waldo Emerson wrote, "A man should learn to detect and watch that gleam of light which flashes across his mind from within."

Joan Didion says that "a shimmer around the edges" leads us to our stories.

Pam Houston uses the term "glimmers" to mean "what grabs my attention." She wrote:

> As I move through the world, I wait to feel something I call a glimmer, a vibration, a little charge of resonance that says, "Hey writer, look over here." I feel it deep in my chest, this buzzing that lets me know this thing I am seeing/hearing/smelling/tasting on the outside is going to help me unlock some part of a story I have on the inside. I keep an ongoing record of these glimmers, writing down not my interpretation of them, not my imagined connection to them, not an emotional contextualization of them, but just the thing itself. Get in, get it down, get out and move on to the next glimmer. Then, when I have some time to write, I read through the glimmer files in my computer and try to find a handful that seem like they will stick together, that when placed in proximity with each other will create a kind of electricity.

Dani Shapiro defined a glimmer as "that sudden, electric sense of knowing" in her book *Still Writing*.

Buhner

I was introduced to this idea of a glimmering thread by Stephen Harrod Buhner, in his book *Ensouling Language*. I pondered the concept for a long time. What was a golden thread? Was it simply an important thing that catches a writer's attention?

Buhner offered his explanation and outlined a pattern that a writer might follow in order to turn a golden thread into a form.

> I'll be doing something, it doesn't matter what, and something will catch my attention, and that thing, whatever it is, is what I then attend to. That moment of captured attention is what I call the touch of a golden thread. These kinds of experiences happen to all of us all the time, but few of us take the time to attend to them....Writers work hard to capture those experiences in language, and in turn, send it on into the world in a new form. It is that *insubstantial thing*, that *livingness* that makes the stories come alive, that makes them mean something that can so deeply touch another human being. Otherwise, it's about extraction and resources, mere form.

Get an idea.

"A golden thread starts with an experience," and "A golden thread may emerge from any ordinary thing and open a doorway into the imaginal, and through it, the mythic." "It's available to everybody," he also said.

Draft.

Now you must get that idea into raw form. You begin by writing down as best you can what you are experiencing. Write in scenes, at the level of the tangible, *this happened, then this happened*. People are walking around doing things.

Shape.

"Then you must shape it into a coherent, layered, luminous, and living work," said Buhner, and "So we work at our craft, work to shape the imaginal that is flowing into a coherent form, work to make it art."

Revise.

Up to now this is the process for any writing. Here's where the method changes.

Buhner describes the system of crafting as one of comparing the feeling of the golden thread to the lines you have written. Does your language do justice to your experience? If not, then tinker until you are as close to this thing as you can be.

In more simple terms, we write down what happened or what we imagined happened, then we read what we write, and we consider how close the written version represents the version in our heads. We continue, back and forth, between the actual lived experience and the representation of that experience.

Find meaning.

The longer you follow the thread, the more meaning you find. As George Washington Carver said, "Anything will give up its secrets if you love it long enough." Or Faulkner, "The deeper the desire, the deeper the story."

Welcome the duende.

Somewhere along the way, from the thread, you make what Buhner calls a "long, floating leap into the unconscious." This is where you find duende. "It is a moment in which a particular kind of experience occurs....You feel a power emanating from the words," he wrote. "A golden thread always leads to such a leap if it is followed; it always generates an experience of duende somewhere in the piece." The longer you follow the thread, the more leaps into the unconscious generate an experience of duende.

Duende

Literally translated, duende means "boss," and also "spirit" or "soul." Plus it's an elf found in Spanish mythology. As used in art, it has been translated to mean "elusive aesthetic" or "transformative power" or "magneto." Poetry can have duende, as can flamenco music or any art. Not all art has it. Duende is art with mystery, with soul.

Spanish poet Federico Garcia Lorca wrote, "The duende, then, is a power, not a work. It is a struggle, not a thought." Lorca defines duende by the presence of four elements:

- irrationality
- earthiness
- a heightened consciousness of death
- a touch of the diabolical.

I wrote about duende extensively in *Wild Spectacle*, in a chapter about Costa Rica called "The Duende of Cabo Blanco." If you want to think about this more deeply, that would be good reading for you.

Read this sentence from Leslie Marmon Silko, one short

quote from her novel *Ceremony*: "But it left something with him; as long as the hummingbird had not abandoned the land, somewhere there were still flowers, and they could all go on."

That line has duende.

Finding duende through craft

Sometimes I get into flow while writing and I make a long, beautiful leap into the unconscious, and the work will take on this quality of duende. Those moments are rare—far too rare—lucky and fleeting. Somewhere in my writing journey, however, I found that I could subvert the floating leap with craft. Something happens in the period of time between getting a rough draft on paper and returning to revise. During this time the conscious and the unconscious mingle. When I revisit a piece, amazing leaps will have happened. That's the current. That's magic.

Ways to slay magic

- Make fun of it.
- Make fun of people who are communicating seriously about it.
- Speak too extensively of a work in progress.
- Fail to keep agreements with yourself, with your muse, and with the dreamer. If you say, "I'm going to write for an hour in the morning," and then you don't, you are slaying magic.
- Expose the magician within you. As Buhner so beautifully writes, "Exposing the dreamer, unprotected, to external and negative forces." This means reviews, critics, bad agents, overbearing editors, and overly negative writing teachers.

- Expose yourself to people who don't like you. I have identified people—sometimes very close to me— who are not able to fully believe in themselves and therefore in others. I limit my time with these good folks, mostly because I am especially susceptible to denigrations and limiting beliefs. When I am obliged to be around such folks, I often carry on two conversations, one with the person and the other with myself, in my head. The person says, "I don't think that's going to work." "Yes, lots of people think that," I will say. In my head I say, "Of course it's going to work." My biggest problem is that I'm a name-caller, sadly, so in my head I really say, "Of course it's going to work, you idiot," then I have to sit myself down and instruct myself to quit the ad hominem attacks. (Why is it so clear that name-calling is an ad hominem attack, while a passive-aggressive limiting belief tossed onto another is not? Anything that makes you feel less loved, less expansive, and less capable is an ad hominem attack.)
- Insult the magician—this means you need to believe that you are mythic, iconic, and archetypal, because you are. Believe in yourself, honor yourself, treat yourself well.

How writing comes alive

- By understanding that your work is with invisibles. The primary thing a writer works with is not words but meanings.
- By consciously working to inhabit words.
- By filling words with meaning.
- By finding a deep interior life.

- By finding words to express the sentiments and feelings in your interior life.
- By moving toward honesty with yourself and with everyone else.

Beyond words

I want to drop in a few last words from my old friend Buhner. "Writing that is merely a human being forcing words into a certain shape without regard for their feelings on the matter is not, and never can be, art." You can call yourself a writer. Nobody is going to stop you. But 95 percent of the writers at work think they are working with words, and with the systems we've developed in our languages for working with words, including grammar, rhetoric, and spelling. To find art you will need to plunge far beyond words.

∾

Exercise

The next time you are out and about, look for a glimmer or a golden thread.

∾

Prompt

What larger idea is calling me?
    What I'm really trying to say is...
    The thing I can't see is...
    The thing you can't see is...

22

WHO DOES AND WHO DOESN'T

It's not how much you want it, it's what you are prepared to give up.
Caryl Phillips, author of *Crossing the River*

Many forces conspire against a writer sitting at her lonely desk day after day. Many forces plot against the book and its consequence in society. Many forces marginalize art.

Therefore, most people never make it. They don't get the book written, or they don't get it published, or they get it published but it's never heard from again.

Quitting is okay

Once I ran into a middle-aged, snazzy woman I recognized. A year previous she had attended an all-day nonfiction workshop I taught in a nearby papermill town.

"How's the writing going?" I asked her.

"Oh, I was hoping you wouldn't recognize me," she said. "I knew you would ask me that."

"You must not be writing."

"I decided not to do it," she said.

"That's okay. Plenty of people enjoy wonderful lives and never write."

"It was too hard," she said. "I saw at your workshop how hard it was going to be. I didn't want to give up that much."

"Good for you," I said. "Most people never realize that. They just keep wishing."

Yes, writing is hard work, but when I'm in flow, when magic is happening, doves being pulled out of handkerchiefs, writing doesn't feel like work.

Who does

Teaching a writing class is a bit like playing the lottery. A teacher never knows what student will actually become a writer—and in my snobby way I'm talking about not just any kind of writer, but a writer of books, a developer of ideas, a thought-leader, a merchant of words. Kittredge talked about this one day in grad school, in an ivory-painted cement-block room filled with metal and plastic chairs on the second floor of the Liberal Arts Building at the University of Montana.

"It's always hard to tell," he said to the class. "Who is going to actually do this." His eyes darted around the room like a pair of crossbills in a streambed. I was studying his body language closely. Kittredge held himself stiffly, sitting in his wooden chair, holding his arms close to his barrel chest, both feet flat on the floor. "I mean, who's going to make it." He emphasized the words *make it*.

I was watching to determine if by chance he was talking to me. "Sometimes a person is outgoing in class, takes notes, turns in good stuff. They leave and I never hear another thing out of them. But I've had quiet people in class never ask questions, leave right afterward, turn in flimsy work. And they make it. I've never figured out how to tell who's going to do it. Sometimes the people who do it surprise me."

He seemed confounded. He seemed to really need to talk about this. So he said it again, "The person in class that you think has the talent, who does the spectacular writing, is usually not the person who goes on and does it. The person who does it is often the one you don't think will."

"I just wait and see," he said. What he was trying to say was, "You're one of the people I'd like to believe in. But I've been so wrong over the years that I don't dare bet on you."

Like Kittredge, I wasn't sure if I'd make it. Like Kittredge, I was waiting. Sometimes the wait is long, not a matter of months or years, but decades, because writing a book that gets picked by others can take a while. In my notes from Kittredge's class I have this line, probably from a visiting speaker. "This is my first book. I've been writing for 16 years." All that time, Kittredge was waiting on her.

I mulled over his comments about "making it." He was also saying that "making it" is a private matter, a battle inside a person, and it has to be fought privately. No classroom can resolve it. No editor can. No luck can. (Well, they help. So does marketing dollars. From research I was shocked to learn how many well-known writers have expensive publicists working for them. By "expensive" I mean $5-10K a month for six months.)

Change your life

Sorry to talk about Kittredge all the time, but he was the teacher I worked with the longest. One thing that he stressed is that your project should be a book. "An essay or a poem won't change your life. A book will change your life." I say this with a caveat, because an old and dear friend who has published over

20 books said to me that none of his books had changed his life. Not one of them had ever sold more than 2,000 copies. He persuaded me to revise Kittredge's philosophy to, A book *can* change your life.

Kittredge's version of "making it" is probably my version. Most of us write for self-healing or self-actualization in our journals, but this work is not necessarily literature. "Making it" is writing for others. Shipping the work, as Seth Godin would say. Being a professional. Being recognized for it. Developing a readership, a group of followers. Getting published in far-reaching venues.

Yet, to acknowledge lots of versions of "making it" seems important, since I myself have never published in New York, and yet I've made it. My dreams have come true.

As a teacher, I've wanted, selfishly, to see my own students publish. I've had wildly gifted writers who I never saw or heard from again. I've had wildly gifted writers who bounced along. I've had gifted ones who rocketed into the limelight, and mildly gifted ones who bounced along. By far, the largest percentage of people, gifted or not, never finish a project, never submit, and never have a chance to rocket.

Piddling

My husband, a visual artist, was for many years a piddler. Over the course of 15 years, since he enrolled in his first art class at the University of Mississippi as a grown man, his skills steadily improved. He had talent on the first day of his first class, but he would complete assignments with the least possible expenditure of energy and refuse to try new techniques and art forms. He wouldn't paint with oils and he wouldn't do portraits, for example. He wouldn't draw teeth.

As the years passed, his biases fell away, and now he's an oil painter doing portraits of people smiling, rows of white teeth.

He paints daily, steadily, passionately. He started entering contests and doing shows and submitting to magazines. Having watched his transformations, I don't say what he will or won't do. Had he been a student in my class, I would not have predicted he would make it.

A single mother, I took Kittredge's class in fall of 1995 and continued to write through the summer of 1996, while my first-grade son spent two months visiting his father in Vermont. I completed the first draft of *Ecology of a Cracker Childhood*, although it was named *Where the Cutting Ends* at that point. In fall of 1996 I printed out the manuscript and timidly asked Kittredge to look at it.

A couple of weeks later he handed it back. "You've got something here," he said. "It's about honor."

I didn't know what he meant.

The following summer Kittredge's partner, Annick Smith, gave me a working scholarship to Yellow Bay Writers Workshop, where I was introduced to literary agent Lizzie Grossman. I took the opportunity to describe my project to her, and she asked me to send it. When I did, she mailed a contract and began to peddle my book around New York. Rejections piled up. Soon Lizzie exhausted her contacts and also her hope for the book, and I accepted that my book would not publish. By then I had finished my MFA in Montana and returned to my grandmother's empty farmhouse in Georgia, owned by my uncle, who didn't mind me living there as long as I nailed back any boards that fell off and acted right. I supported myself with freelance jobs, enough to scrape by. I had a few thousand in student loan debt to repay.

One day the phone rang. Emilie Buchwald, founding editor of Milkweed Editions, was on the line. "Bill Kittredge told me that you have a manuscript I might be interested in," she said.

"Well," I said. "I do have a manuscript. It's with my agent but it hasn't sold."

"Would you have your agent send it to me?"

"Most definitely," I said. "Thank you for wanting to look at it."

"Bill said it has potential," she said.

Hurray to Kittredge for stressing from Day 1 of class to aim toward a book. Hurray to him for teaching me about scenes. Hurray to him for loving a woman who organized writing workshops. Hurray to him for telling Emilie about me.

Hurray to me for writing the book.

What keeps me going

Some years ago Jeremy B. Jones of the Southern Nature Writers Project, which was directed by Dorinda Dallmeyer and John Lane, interviewed me about nature writing. Jones went on to publish *Bearwallow: A Personal History of a Mountain Homeland.*

"How do you manage to write so beautifully and clearly about something you love that is being threatened, without being overwhelmed by fear and anger?" Jones asked.

I am often overwhelmed by fear and anger. I get hopeless. Two things keep me going.

One of those is the idea of service. The climate crisis and war and injustice may be gigantic, but I can't *not* do anything about them. I want to go to my grave (and I plan for it to be a grave, since cremation uses too much fossil fuel) knowing that I never stopped trying, that I did everything I could to protect and uphold life.

As an environmental writer part of what keeps me going is the knowledge that the bulk of environmental destruction, like societal disintegration, has happened in very recent history. Our rampant use of chemicals in agriculture, for example, only began after World War II. Until around 1940 nobody saw a pine plantation in the South. Gasoline-powered vehicles are barely 100 years old. So, you see, having been born in 1962 and reared in an impoverished region, I can almost remember a time before chemical farming, before rampant tree-cutting, before widespread plastics, before people began fleeing rural areas. My mother definitely remembers farming with mules and manure and home-saved seeds.

A part of me thinks then, if all this terrible destruction started so recently, surely we can reverse it. Surely it's not part of a permanent disintegration.

Jones also asked me, "To what do you attribute your persistence and commitment to service?

"To love," I said. And love is a formidable force.

I hope you find something that keeps you going until you make it.

Exercise

Write about what keeps you going.

Prompt

To what or to whom do you devote your writing?

PART III

23

HOW TO MAGIC

I began to write about the mysterium while preparing to teach one summer at Bread Loaf Environmental Writers Workshop near Ripton, Vermont. Soon after I arrived I walked the Robert Frost Trail, and I happened upon this couplet from a Frost poem:

> *We dance round and a ring and suppose.*
> *But the Secret sits in the middle and knows.*

It's everywhere

As I was reading the essays of some of the participants, I came upon interesting excerpts which, with permission, I have pulled.

> ....Maybe you don't believe me, that I can feel the soil, I don't blame you, these are not knowledges the world easily approves of. But what if we did approve? What if we said yes, this is something I can feel, every living thing that is next to me, and who is next to them and to them and to them?

—Marie Turner

What followed is difficult to explain, or to overstate the significance of. I felt myself dissolve into the whole scene: the meditation hall, the field, the benches—the other meditators, the sun, the deer fearlessly grazing the apple trees. I became all of it—became the mountain Tahoma.

—Christopher Densmore

My point is, examples of this knowing and unknowing are everywhere. Maybe they're not in the grant files of the National Science Foundation, but they are everywhere else. Magic happens, whether you believe it or not, leaving mysteries that cannot be explained away.

Unheard-of point of view

Part of the reason I fell in love with the fourth genre, creative nonfiction, was because of personal narrative, which allows the pronoun "I." So much can be done with it; so many gaps can be filled and modern literature has been doing a great job with that. Using first person, a writer no longer has to hide, but can be a fully seen and fully realized narrator: The first-person voice in creative nonfiction is truth-telling, as in, *I want to tell you what life has been like.*

Third person, of course, has its own power and strength, especially for fiction. Third-person omniscience allows the writer to see what, far below, is going on in the world. William Faulkner and Harry Crews and Flannery O'Connor and Alice Walker and my favorite, Willa Cather, barely used the pronoun "I," at least not for *I*, and they were able to reach fantastic places. The third-person voice is an avenue of empathy, as in, *Here's how they were feeling.*

Some literature, however, goes someplace else entirely, far

beyond the first-person's depth of self-exploration and the third-person's omniscience. Consider if you will this poem by Rilke:

> *I live my life in widening circles*
> *that reach out across the world.*
> *I may not complete this last one*
> *but I give myself to it.*
> *I circle around God, around the primordial tower.*
> *I've been circling for thousands of years*
> *and I still don't know: am I a falcon,*
> *a storm, or a great song?*

Rilke is not in the truth-telling "I" world. He is not in the empathetic third-person, he-she-and-they world. Rilke is in another world. He has made of himself a vessel; he is trying to find the god in the story. The point of view here is sacred. So the question might be: *What invisible forces caused this?*

The world, I think, needs less identity-based "I," and less people-splaining "he," "she," and "they." It needs more of this other thing, a soul grappling with what it means to be human in a blown-apart world. Archetypes are not a thing of the past, and neither is myth. We are mythic, archetypal beings. The context has disappeared, not the thing itself.

If you want to get there

Let's look at the ways mystics get closer to the nonlocal realm so that you have some avenues for pursuing magic.

They remove themselves from human community, away to mountaintops or jungles.

They spend time outside, grounding and sunning and paying attention to the animate earth.

They go on silent walks.

They sit in silence.

They fast. Fast 36 hours by waking up one morning and not eating all day. Sleep again and eat when you wake the next morning. Do this on the equinoxes and solstices. Or once a year on a special day. The longest I have fasted is 10 days, only water. I'm not sure how healthy this was. I was a bit desperate. I was desperate to turn off the needs of the body in an attempt to listen to spirit. I'll also note that fasting has become more difficult as I've aged. These days it requires that I give myself completely to it, and I don't do it very often.

They limit the distractions of material possessions.

They wear one type of garment, often simple.

They wear items of red clothing to repel negative energy.

They push the limits of suffering.

They pray.

They meditate, practicing how to turn down and shut off the busyness of the mind.

They create a labyrinth for walking meditations.

They practice yoga, especially with an older teacher who is very wise. Meditating is easier when the body is engaged.

They practice understanding the kind of person they want to spend time with. They begin to spend time with people who are deeply trustworthy, deeply kind, deeply nourishing, deeply loving.

They build altars. On it they place rocks and pebbles, feathers, bird nests, important books, candles, crystals, incense, affirmations. On mine is a letter from my son, pine cones, three carved peach pits given to me by a security guard, two tarot decks, I Ching coins, sometimes $100 bills.

They listen to trees. I mean really listen. I go sit under a tree and turn on my feeling sense. I open the chambers of my heart, and I give the tree my full attention. I listen for any message that is not coming from my own busy mind.

They use plant medicine. They believe in the deep and

powerful healing energy of plants, because over and over plants have healed folks, even when Western medicine could not.

They listen to babies. When I am around babies, I try to really listen to how they are doing and attempt not to impose my needs on them.

They listen to animals. When I am around animals, I try to really listen to how they are doing.

They honor the ancestors. Once I saw a ghost. Well, now that I think about it, twice I saw a ghost. In both cases the person had committed suicide. One was an ex-boyfriend who died by hanging and the other was a veteran who had lived in the historic farmhouse that we purchased and who died by gunshot. I saw both of them only peripherally and only briefly. I recognized one immediately, since I had known him intimately, and the other I later identified from an old photo. I have come, like some cultures, to believe that our ancestors walk among us, in some form. Some cultures don't pray to god but to their ancestors to intercede for them. I ask my ancestors to intercede for me. So do your genealogy. Learn who your ancestors were, even if all you can uncover is their names. Sketch out a family tree, or print one from online and fill it out. Do your DNA. Display photos of your ancestors. Write about your ancestors. Visit their graves. Respect cemeteries. Clean cemeteries.

They do not needlessly kill any form of life. They try not to kill spiders. Some cultures believe that spiders are our ancestors. If this is true, then tons of my ancestors have come to live with me.

They pray. Fly prayer flags. They spin prayer wheels.

They burn candles, which are like post-it notes for me. They remind me of the intentions I am putting out into the ether.

They try psychedelics. (Please, don't do anything stupid. Don't poison yourself. Use a guide.)

They pay attention to dreams. As Maya Angelou said, "Dreams can tell people all sorts of things. They can work out problems. Especially for writing. Maybe if a writer is hesitant to get to a depth in a character...the brain says, 'Okay, you go on to sleep. I'll take care of it. I'll show you'...There's a phrase in West Africa called 'deep talk.' Meaning you can continue to go down deeper and deeper. Dreams may be deep talk." I encourage myself to dream. I think about dreams. I write them down.

They divine. They work with the tarot, throw the I Ching, and consult an astrologer. I too use these tools to help me figure myself out.

Rewilding

Because the universe is the source and home of all energies, all spiritual connections, and all magic, and because the earth is our home within the universe, and because earth-based cultures are also the most magical, we have to return ourselves to the wildness from which we came. This means reattaching with deeper bonds to our places and also to the planet.

As good a word as any for this is "rewilding."

I work hard to rewild myself, so that my work smells of wildness. The wildness comes, if I am lucky, in the form of a touch of genius, a gushing flow of creativity, a lush animation, and a fierce energy. I am not saying that I always get there, only that I keep trying.

In ecology rewilding means rebuilding diversity and abundance.

In life rewilding means

- grounding
- reconnecting with the songlines and the energies of the earth

- reconnecting ourselves with the energies of each other, strange as they can be
- regularly discharging the energies of the internet
- decolonizing the Western mind, becoming native to place again

In writing rewilding means all of the above—decolonizing the Western mind, rebuilding diversity and abundance, and becoming native to place again. (You will find a list of ways to rewild in the Appendix.)

Mysterium

As a writer, you can magic in all the ways that anyone ever has. Freewriting as Peter Elbow prescribed it is a great start for dropping out of the rational mind and into feeling mind. If you too would like to approach the primordial tower in *your* work, if you would like to be mythic and archetypal, then start by doing some flow-writes. You can become adept at Buhner's feeling sense, practicing it as you move through the world. You can magic by rewilding yourself.

Best wishes

That is what I know about transcendence, the flash of epiphany, the glimmer of a golden thread, the duende. You can see that most of it I learned from others, who I attribute with congealing these ideas in my head and body and setting me on fire. Now you're on your own with studying the mysterium and exploring ways to gain passage into and through it. I wish you the best of luck in seeking and finding what cannot be found but nonetheless exists.

≈

Exercise

1. Choose one item on the above list and pursue it today.
2. Write a scene about something inexplicable that happened to you.

Prompt

1. I feel magic when I am...
2. On my altar is...

24

CAPTAIN

M uch as I detest this particular metaphor, I am an empire-builder. I want more books, more money, bigger audiences, a longer reach, grander awards, bigger print-runs, more visible results. For a couple of decades I couldn't articulate that. I also want fewer trees cut and more ecosystems saved and less carbon dioxide in the atmosphere. Coming to terms with what it meant to be an "empire-builder" and also an environmentalist was slow.

One thing was slower, and that was coming to terms with being both an empire-builder and a woman.

I had gone to Montana when the West was at a crossroads. The West was romantically built on the idea of the cowboy, a myth that Larry McMurtry tried to snuff out once and for all in his essay, "Take My Saddle from the Wall." Although McMurtry dug the grave of the last cowboy in September 1968, when that essay published in *Harper's,* the idea of cowboyhood lives on. Meanwhile, a platoon of big male writers sprang out of the West or had ties to the West or finally went West. Hemingway had gone to Ketchum, Idaho when the sea got too deep and Africa too far. The big guys, people like Jim Harrison and

Richard Ford and Tom McGuane and Rick Bass, owned Montana.

In his book *The Accidental Life*, Terry McDonell talks about soliciting these guys to write for him, guys who were living as big as they were writing. Tom McGuane called it "having a long reach," a phrase I don't really understand, which is why I'm using it. Would these men be called "influencers" now? Americans exchanged the romance of the cowboy for that of the larger-than-life outdoorsman.

I was not a larger-than-life outdoorsman. I hardly had any reach at all. I was a young single mother climbing out of a colorful but crippling childhood, trying to be a nature writer, pulled toward something I didn't understand and which possibly had no place for me.

Our movements

I believe that we have two or three great issues we grapple with our entire lives. I call them *movements*. One of Kittredge's movements was longing for a place he could not actually live. He was born in cowboy country, but built to be a writer and a scholar. The two forces were irreconcilable inside him.

One movement for me is the sense of belonging or not belonging. Did I belong to my birth family? Did I belong in grad school? Did I belong in the decidedly male American letters? Did I belong on social media? Do I belong in wilderness?

Wild women

By the time I arrived to Montana in 1995, the writing world was different from the one Hemingway exited in 1961. Women had appeared on the range. Terry Tempest Williams made a name for herself in 1991 with her breakaway book, *Refuge,* and many other women writers were burning like candles on trails. They were trail-blazing the mountains. Gretel Ehrlich listened to the wind in Wyoming. Kathleen Norris was somewhere in Dakota, Ann Zwinger in Colorado, Annie Proulx in Wyoming. Women were traipsing and hunting and canoeing. They weren't yet in the magazines, at least not often and not enough, but they were leaving their kitchens to head afield.

Because nature writing was opening up to women and because Kittredge was different than his prototypes (although he could outdrink them), I got a chance. Kittredge took the work of his students, women or men, seriously. He took me seriously. I probably owe that to Annick. Strong-willed, independent, forward-thinking, radical, gorgeous, Annick changed Bill's thinking more than anyone, I believe. By the time they met she was as famous as he. The two of them collaborated on the Montana anthology, *The Last Best Place,* as well as the movie, with Robert Redford, *A River Runs through It.* I think that once Bill had fallen in love with Annick, he was in love with all powerful women and their stories. He signed off one letter to me with "Stay tough and smart."

Besides, he'd been teaching for at least three decades and he had realized that his male writers didn't always make it. Sometimes the female writers were the ones who did.

I'd been reared a woman from the beleaguered South, and being a Southern woman comes with a particular suitcase of societal stereotypes and personal crosses. I learned to recognize injustice when I was very young. I kept my own name when I married and tried not to let being a woman stop me from doing what I damn well pleased. I drove a truck. I changed my own tires. I changed my own oil.

Even as a feminist, however, I struggled to find my voice, to rid myself of shame, to put my desires first, to strategize. Plus, I was a nature writer, which at that time insured marginalization in the literary world, and the line between marginalization as a nature writer and marginalization as a woman blurred.

Clarity

I would have thought little about this were it not for a question someone asked me publicly. I had published my first book and perhaps my second. One day in a Q&A at Berry College, which hosted the Southern Women Writers Conference for years, someone stood up.

"Has being a woman held you back?"

I answered with all the honestly possible at the time, that no, being a woman had not cramped or stifled or silenced or bound me. I had been the driver of my own wagon. I had always steered.

I was proud to say that.

The question, however, followed me home. *Had* being a woman held me back as a writer?

A more true answer

Years later, actually when I read McDonell's book, I could finally answer. Yes, at the time I came of age as a writer, being a woman held me back.

1. Like a woman-owned company I could fill a position. I could rep the South and womanhood and poverty. *Ecology* won an American Book Award in 2000, which goes to books that represent diversity—of race, sex, creed, and cultural origin— without regard to the size of the press or the genre. How many times have I been the only woman on a panel, in an anthology, at a reading? How easy it was for organizers to have me there.

2. Like Ruth in the Bible, I was good. I was cheerful, friendly, even apologetic. I was happy with what I got. I felt as if

I earned what I got and nothing else. I was not going to ask for more.

3. Like all women, especially ovulating ones, I had a sexuality to exploit.

4. And like any woman, especially of child-bearing age, I had a sexuality to *overcome*. The gravity of this sunk into me after I'd read a number of John McPhee's books, trying not to feel jealous that anything he wrote published first in *The New Yorker* then in book form, until he had dozens of titles. The epiphany came after I finished "A Forager," a telling portrait of Euell Gibbons. McPhee had arranged to trek with Gibbons for a week, I think it was, first on the Susquehanna River and then the Appalachian Trail, foraging along the way and eating off the land, 16 wild-crafted meals. Could I, as a woman, dial up Euell Gibbons and invite him camping for a week?

Women not allowed

Detractors of my stand are already thinking, *Of course you could have done this*. You could have invited a friend along. You could have invited Euell's wife. You could have invited a photographer.

Yes and yes and yes. The fact remains that issues of sexuality are real, and the burden of them is placed more squarely on the woman—to deflect, to clarify, to avoid, to stymie, to fake, to accept, to escalate, to profess, to succumb.

Detractors can also say that we design our lives. *You are where you want to be*, my doctor tells me. In many ways we choose; in many ways we don't. Women have been able to find ways to live outside societal norms. They've dressed as men, refused to marry, taken male pen names, played sports, used birth control, had abortions, wandered off into wilderness alone. However, in other aggressive ways we don't choose our lives. I think of a Middle Eastern woman who was raped but then stoned to death by her brothers.

When I read McDonell's book, the same time I was revisiting McPhee's body of work, I discovered that I knew or had met a number of the writers with whom McDonell worked. Most of them he invited on an adventure—to shoot, to golf, to hunt, to watch ballgames, to paddle, to hike, to party, to whatever. I think of the men's club. The hunt club. Any all-male society.

In too many ways writing has been a society of men.

Like my mother, I had a house to take care of, meals to cook, laundry to wash, a child to raise. Like my mother, I could not afford a housekeeper. Unlike my mother, I was, for over two decades, the head of my household and its breadwinner—first as a single person, then as a single parent, then as a wife by circumstances of my husband's career. Unlike my mother, I was an artist.

On fire

After my sixth book, *The Seed Underground*, I quit writing for a while.

Writing the book had taken me three years and I'd been paid an advance of $4,500. The book's text was seed diversity, a subject I've been obsessed with since childhood, and I was working with one of my favorite publishers, Chelsea Green, and with a stellar editor, Brianne Goodspeed. The book won five or six national awards and was translated into French and Turkish. It got my picture in tons of newspapers and magazines.

Yet my income hovered at poverty level. Royalties weren't flowing into my bank account. I didn't have health insurance. I was hearing of other writers, men and women, in similar situations. Anyone could understand that book-writing, for me and for most people, wasn't working.

So I decided to stop.

I tried.

But writing was like a flame inside me that began to rage. I was burning up. I arrived at my writing desk burning, and I burned until other responsibilities pried me from my chair. I was up before dawn and working until bedtime, which in my house is 10 p.m. The fire would not go out. It got hotter. So I accepted penury, at least at that moment, because being a writer offered so much, a stab at affecting transformation in people's lives, in the environment, and in the world.

The burning I feel—that is a gift.

For five years I taught a weekend workshop at an inn in the Blue Ridge Mountains of northern Georgia. Planning the fifth summer, the organizer and I decided to invite only past attendees. That workshop would be a retreat where the participants would do their own writing, I would not have to teach all day, I could do my work and be present to check in with them. I scheduled mornings for writing time, then afternoons for craft talks, private meetings, and workshopping.

The first morning I took my notebook to a table on a wide porch that runs the length of the inn so I could look out into a gigantic red oak that is always hopping with phoebes and warblers. As usual, I was burning. Sometimes the fire burns like gasoline has been thrown on it, all-consuming, and sometimes it burns like winking embers.

I couldn't help but notice that the other writers were not burning. They were piddling, chatting, taking little walks, biding their time, wasting time.

I had a sharp and sad realization. Sometimes we see passion and we want that passion. We want to touch it and own a piece of it. But passion does not come from without. It comes from within. You have a flame, you feed it, it grows and grows.

It's eternal. You don't burn by standing next to someone who does.

Standing next to such a human conflagration, you see the person is on fire. That kind of burning is an awesome thing. I especially love being on fire and standing next to someone else who is also on fire. I strategize how to sit beside these people.

Fires can increase in intensity. I have, for example, watched my husband's fire growing. Fires can be fed.

Money

I accepted penury until I didn't.

Story as a deal

When I was young, I recognized my father as the greatest salesman in the world. To him, the deal was more important than anything. If he wanted an old pistol, for example, he would figure out a way to get it. He was going to get it at his price. He wanted to complete the deal, no matter what, and to win. People have told me they felt my father always got the better of them. They always felt, at the end of dealing, that they lost and he won.

Once my friend Dink NeSmith, newspaperman, sent me a recording of Buddy Jewell's song, "I Just Wanna Thank Everone Who Ever Told Me No." "This is my theme song," he said. He told me a story of a piece of land he wanted. He visited the landowner many times, inquiring about purchasing this land, and each time she refused. Each time he heard "no," he wanted this property more than ever. One day when he went to visit, everything had changed. The landowner wanted to sell, a change of heart that Dink attributed to not giving up.

I ask myself of a story, *What do I need to do to complete this deal? What can I do to turn a "no" into "yes?"*

As a woman writer I've learned a few amazing lessons and strategies.

I'm seldom spending time moving a boulder out of my way. I'm figuring out a way to go around it.

I'm not waiting. To hell with being a good and faithful servant, a Ruth, a bonbon, a team player, a convenience, a position to fill.

I'm not being quiet.

Our own blocks

Sometimes the boulder in our way is ourselves. We get in our own way, we don't show up. We get scared. We talk ourselves out of wanting the thing.

One summer I led a series of goal-setting exercises with a group of writers. I asked them, *What are you doing that you don't need to do?* They said,

- Looking often at my cell phone
- Being so many people's "person"
- Going online first thing in the morning
- Procrastinating (I've perfected techniques.)
- Reading about time management
- Committing to professional duties, not to my art
- Checking the phone first thing
- Worrying about other people

When I became an empire-builder my actions changed. My tone changed. My responses changed. My fee changed. Who I associated with changed. What I said changed. What I tolerated changed. What I wanted changed. What I expected changed. What I heard changed.

Tooness

Any adjective followed by "too" arouses my suspicion. My sister has always been much prettier than I, and when we were young, I often heard that I was "pretty too." (I'm sure she heard that she was "smart too.") Not long ago I was invited to lunch. "Kristy is coming over," my friend said, "and I wanted you to know you can come too."

"Come too" is not an invitation. That is guilt.

Maybe it was a rhetorical *faux pas*, but rhetoric is my world, and recognizing "tooness" has been life-changing. I'm not interested in coming too or succeeding too or winning too. I'll be riding six white horses when I come. I'll be wearing a crown. Hundred-dollar bills will be flying out of the golden carriage.

Hard as the reality is to swallow, some people in our society work hard and are not rewarded for it. Others are lazy and *are* rewarded. Some get rewarded for other people's work. Some are rewarded for criminal behavior, especially thievery. Some are rewarded for destructive behaviors.

I may be an empire-builder, but I'm a hard worker and I work for the rewards I receive—and I say all this to give you my hard-boiled advice: *If you are a piddler and you enjoy piddling, piddle. If you understand that and accept it, you're ahead of the game. You can go to writing workshops and retreats and support groups and book clubs, and you can be the person you want to be. Piddling, however, is not embers at the root, flaring at the crown. If you want to burn like that, you've got to feed the fire.*

How

First, show up. As I've said, showing up is more than half the battle.

Other wealth

Let me add one thing: What I have sought more than fame or fortune is community, and intimacy, and meaning, and deep relationship. In that matrix I am a very rich person. Writing has afforded me a chance at an inconceivable level of community; a chance for my ramshackle life to have meaning; and a chance for deeper relationships and greater intimacy with people I admire and respect, especially writers, editors, biologists, naturalists, and people of all stripes who just plain *care*. That means more to me than empire.

Exercise

Name at least one movement (larger issue) that you grapple with. Add it to your list of obsessions.

Prompt

As a (woman, man, nonbinary) writer...

25

STORMY WEATHER

The writing world is constructed of walls, hoops, locked doors, and mazes, and it is loud with din and clamor as you try to find your way through it. You're going to run into disappointment. You're going to wonder why things don't get easier, after all the sacrifice and pain.

Bad news comes often to a serious writer, and for that you will need a plan for recovery. Resilience will be important, because you'll suffer losses. I could paper a wall with rejection letters. But I don't.

I focus on our human ability to withstand adversity, the strength and speed of our resistance to impact. I consider what else I'm willing to give up.

I have learned to have a back-up plan and a backup's backup, to never be torn loose from any mooring like a heavy boat in a storm, never to be without bumpers hanging alongside, never without a rope bow and stern. I think how not to take things personally. I think of who to tell and who not to tell. I think of where to go next, of whom to approach next, of who has a door open, not blocking that door but standing to the side, welcoming. I'm thinking of a plan.

Less and less I think of how to get picked but how to pick myself.

Jump back

Loss has a cycle: shock, recovery, shock, recovery.

Resilience means "to jump back." It's moss springing back, bluebirds laying another round of eggs, a stump sprouting. Resilience is showing up, trying again, starting anew, not accepting no, looking for yes, asking again, signing up, sending a manuscript out for the fortieth time, figuring out another way to make something happen.

Truly, however, resilience is not an action but a habit cultivated inside.

Once I heard a securities trader talk about ways to weather an economic crash. He said you'd need silver and gold since paper would become worthless. You'd need cash in small bills. You'd need to be debt-free. You'd need alcohol, because people always want a drink. You'd need tools and real skills. You'd need the ability to research. You'd need how-to books.

Likewise, what will *you* need to survive a crash? How will you jump back from heartbreak? Friends, therapy, hobbies, aware breathing, yoga, antidepressants, walking, cooking, eating, flowers, chocolate, prayer. It's called creative sustainability.

Be aware, too, that privilege makes us resilient. Think about privilege so that you can better understand those without it. If you are a poor writer, a woman writer, a black writer, a state-educated writer, a LGBTQ writer, a Native writer, a Cajun writer, a blind writer, a physically challenged writer, a traumatized writer (and so many more), you will need more creative sustainability than writers who are not these things.

Rejections

One night Simmons Buntin, cofounder of the startup literary magazine *Terrain*, now a leading venue for nature writing, dropped into my online nature-writing course to talk about how a person might publish in *Terrain*'s pages. Someone came up to him at a conference, he said, and asked a seemingly innocent question, "How many times should a person keep submitting to a magazine before giving up?"

Simmons didn't realize he was being set up. "I think you should keep submitting," he told her. "Until your heart is no longer in it." Turns out she had submitted to *Terrain* nine times without success.

"We're all going to get rejections," he said. "I still get rejections. It's the nature of it."

A rejection, he continued, may be less about the quality of the work than what an editor likes/doesn't like or needs/doesn't need. That's why you keep hearing about a piece getting rejected by 17 or 18 editors before getting accepted.

"Keep the faith," Simmons said, "and try not to let rejections get you down."

Good news comes

Giving up is easy. It shapeshifts into many forms, including distractions, procrastinations, ratcheted-down goals, compromises, new preoccupations. It becomes the urge to check the phone, to make a coffee, to take a walk. Sometimes giving up is necessary. However, however, however, if you have a dream and it burns inside you and you wake each morning thinking about it and you go to bed each night dreaming of it, then don't mind the bad news. Bad news comes.

So does the good.

So make goals

A surprising number of people hate goals. If you, however, have decided that you're not a piddler and that you want to design your life, especially around writing, then I advise you not to underestimate goal-setting. It should not be restricted to New Year's Resolutions but should become a daily routine, remembering what you want and what you do to get there. Painter and entrepreneur Jose Trujillo sets outrageous, magnified goals and rewrites them twice a day, morning and night, he once said, in order to stay focused.

When you set your goals, keep them on the down-low. Studies have shown that success releases certain chemicals in our brains, and we set goals because we want to enjoy those volcanic highs. When we *speak aloud* a goal, these exact chemicals get released, and if we are speaking excessively we can lose enthusiasm and momentum for actually achieving the goal. So be circumspect about how loudly and how often you talk. Talk to yourself. Show up and do the work. You will be better served by the goals if they are process-oriented, if they corral you to show up. Read Seth Godin's *The Practice* for inspiration.

Below is a list of prompts for goal-setting:

WHAT IS NEXT FOR ME?

(I suppose I'm going to have to put in time at my desk, every morning, even an hour. 6-7? 7-8? 6-9? It will be easier when R goes back to school.)

WHAT CAN I DO DAILY?

(I really do need to work at my desk every morning and keep working on the clutter and also think hard about sending out and actually get stuff off to editors and publishers. I can be more serious. I

can love myself anyway. I can determine not to write anything new but only work on the pieces I've abandoned. I can Always Be Finishing Something.)

A YEAR FROM NOW, I'D LIKE...

(*To have a cleaner office—I don't dare say perfect—and another book coming out, maybe abandon the novel. I'd really like a group-think to help jumpstart that book—what will its structure be? Themes?*)

WHAT I NEED TO GET THIS DONE.

(*I need to get out of my own way. I need to love being in my office. I need to not feel so alone there. I need to enjoy the persona of writer and the writing itself. I need good health, a plan to exercise later in the day.*)

WHAT AM I DOING THAT I DON'T NEED TO BE DOING?

(*I'm doing too much that someone else could do better. Plenty of people can garden better than I. Pay them to weed.*)

WHAT AM I WILLING TO GIVE UP IN ORDER TO GET WHAT I WANT?

(*I'll give up friends, I'll give up fun excursions with my family, I'll give up social visits, I'll give up movies, I'll give up yoga classes, I'll give up bread-baking, I'll give up a clean house. Or not.*)

Exercise

1. Set aside the next 30 minutes and flow-write answers to the questions above.
2. Go ahead now and make a plan. How do you survive heartbreak? Label a page in your journal "My Resilience." At the top list 10 things you do to reduce anxiety, become re-centered, and feel powerful. Then list five friends you can call if things get bad. Make sure that you're willing to take a call in return from each of those folks when things get bad for them.

Prompt

1. Even for writing, I'll never give up ___
2. Please help me...

26

WELLSPRING

I've been asked how I balance writing, giving talks, caring for my family, and working on my farm?

I write in the early mornings and spend the rest of the day doing everything else—running my writing business, cooking, gardening, canning, cleaning, and anything else that comes up. I do some community organizing, which is a counterpoint in that it takes my mind off my little sphere. When I travel, my husband takes care of everything farmwise and homewise. I'm grateful to have a partner in this venture and specifically to have him. If we both go away, we hire a farmsitter.

Writing as a side-hustle

People arrive to writing from varied circumstances. Some are trying to balance a harried lifestyle with a creative one. Some have to complete reports and plan for classes and arrange childcare or pet care before they take an absence to write. Some arrive with ideas sparking, some need space to develop them. Some need time to wash away other voices that tug at them and to become immersed in the serenity of their writing space and, in turn, to access their deepest emotions and their art.

My advice is, *do what it takes.*

Frame

To use a dance metaphor, how does a writer find their frame and maintain it?

Unfortunately, I find myself saying "no" a lot. No to entering the burger-cooking contest. No to doing a talk for the Garden Club. No to taking a workshop on exotic invasive plants. No to going fishing. No to accepting a real job. No to walking the dogs as much as they'd like to be walked. No to doing my 200th blurb. Our dreams require that we be exceedingly conservative with what we do with our precious time.

Brain health

My father was diagnosed with and died of Alzheimer's, the incidence of which has increased exponentially, and as a survivor of Lyme disease, which can damage the brain, I give a lot of attention to brain health. If our brains are not working well, we can't write well.

Of course the brain can only be as healthy as the body. Diet is extremely important. Avoid sugar as much as possible. Gluten is increasingly inflammatory for many people. Eat live foods, mostly vegetables and greens. Chemicals like Roundup, now widespread, are being implicated in brain dysfunction and other autoimmune illnesses. Buy organic when at all possible. Figure out ways to obtain it.

Science is reporting that humans need to eat good fats, especially since the brain is mostly fatty tissue. This will be avocadoes, coconut oil, olive oil, and raw nuts, which are acceptable to vegetarians and vegans. Omnivores can take fish oil, the best on the market, as well as fats from grassfed animals, including healthy lard. Butter is more healthful if it's organic and also turned into ghee, which removes milk solids. I'm so crazy about using good fat that I slather it on vegetables. I put fat on salads. Sometimes I melt fat (cream, coconut oil, ghee) into my coffee.

I'm no expert on any of this and I'm no medical doctor, but I do take seriously the epidemic of cognitive decline. I would like to remain as sharp as possible for as long as possible. I also acknowledge that some of Western medicine would disagree with adding fat to a diet. Consult a medical advisor you trust.

My serious writer friends take brain supplements like gingko, gotu kola, GABA, theanine, ashwaganda, CoQ10, and cayenne (opens blood vessels) for brain health. Ginger and turmeric cut down on inflammation, including brain inflammation, as do fish oils. Deficits of vitamins C, D and B12 have been insinuated in dementia. Again, consult a medical advisor you trust.

In addition, I'd say eliminate as much stress as you can. Get exercise. Any bilateral (cross-body) movement is supposed to help the brain. This includes something as simple as swinging your arms while walking. One good cross-body exercise, taught to me by Anita Blackwell: Cross arms over chest. Pinch opposite ear lobes. Do squats while bending quickly from the waist, 10 times, blowing out hard each time. Anita recommends doing these before a test or any kind of endurance session.

Sleep

To need sleep and deny yourself is almost criminal. To want to sleep and be unable to do so is terrible. Here are ways to improve sleep—

1. Allow yourself eight hours. Sleep at night. Set a bedtime for yourself and stick to it.

2. Sleep in total darkness, if possible, since any amount of light at night inhibits melatonin production. Speaking of melatonin, 10 mg slow-release is better than sleeping pills.

3. The single most important thing I've done to sleep well is to quit eating at least four hours before bedtime. For some reason the production of insulin causes me to sleep poorly. I try to neither eat or drink after 6 p.m., within reason, with a bedtime of 10 p.m. This has been seriously effective.

4. The next best thing I've done to get a full night of rest, in order to wake up contented, at peace, and without anxiety or fear is to mouth-tape. Mouth-taping is what it sounds like. I place a three-inch length of hypoallergenic tape across my mouth just before I fall asleep. This forces me to breathe through my nose. The first night I did it I was pretty sure I was going to suffocate, although I'd done a tremendous amount of research. I slept all night long and woke up feeling incredible. Literally within one night I was sold. Sometimes now I fall asleep before I remember to tape my mouth, and I regret those nights. The difference is stunning and remarkable. Yet, because it's so weird, I can't really go around proselytizing about mouth-taping. But I'm telling you. If it works, send me $100 dollars. Because that's how you'll be feeling.

5. Employ an electronic sundown, which means shutting off electronic devices at least an hour before bedtime.

6. Do screen fasts, long periods when you aren't in front of a screen. Also, blue-light-blocking glasses can help eliminate the screen effect.

7. However, amber-colored sunglasses filter out the blue wavelength of light, and this inhibits melatonin, which of course you need.

8. Try chamomile tea.

9. The smell of lavender is restful.

10. A writer friend told me to put my legs up against the wall before bed. I can't remember why it helps but I'm adding it.

11. Most people won't go this far, but I turn off the electricity to my house at night. I do this at the breaker box. Night is when a person's parasympathetic nervous system is most active, and I don't want the weird electrical energies rolling around my bedroom. Our house lends itself to this, since it's a vernacular design where the kitchen is separate from the main house. The refrigerator is in the kitchen, and the electricity stays on there, so we don't have to worry about food ruining. We're not always able to cut off every circuit in the main house—in summers we keep a fan aimed at our bed, since we don't have heat and AC there—so that breaker stays on.

Consult a medical advisor you trust, especially one who realizes that some medicines have helped people for thousands of years before industrial medicine came along.

Tricks to stimulate creative thought

The color red provokes thinking. I knew a public relations guy once who painted the walls red in the room where his employees met to brainstorm. Listen to Mozart.

The eyes

Don't forget your eyes. The 20/20/20 Rule is that every 20 minutes you look 20 feet away for 20 seconds. This is one reason my desk faces a window. (Another is that I like watching birds.)

∼

Exercise

Go take a walk of at least 20 minutes.

Prompt

Why I love my body...

27

GOLD COIN

There's an unspoken rule made for writers that we're not supposed to talk about money. We're supposed to be glad we are actually making any money at all. The trope of the starving artist is no joke, with thousands of examples to prove it.

Money oppression requires silence. You don't talk salaries. You don't talk costs. You don't talk profit. Writers don't talk advances. They don't talk fees. They don't talk honoraria.

I obeyed all the rules for a long time, but now I don't.

I want to talk to you about book deals that I've heard about recently.

Advance #1

A talented writer friend who took my course in creative nonfiction wrote me an ecstatic email. "With everything from our class in mind, as well as at my mother's urging, I polished up a proposal to a university press, sent it Saturday, and the editor called me this morning. Like, called me on the phone! He was clearly excited...saying he thought it would fit perfectly into their list. My heart flew right out of my chest."

She had a book deal!

A few days later I heard from the writer again. She had received the contract, which turned out to be a Memorandum of Agreement. This legal agreement gives the publisher the right to refuse the manuscript once it's finished, if he doesn't like it or if he doesn't get peer approval. If he likes the manuscript, the terms are "surprisingly low," as my friend told me. To be exact, the terms are a $500 advance, payable on acceptance, and 7% royalties. The press gets audio and other rights.

That is a "deal" I would not accept.

Advance #2

That week I had another conversation with a friend who writes cookbooks. For their most recent cookbook they received an advance of $100K.

Now they want to do another cookbook, so they contacted a respected agent, who said she won't sell a book unless she gets an advance of $200K. That was shocking. I know these deals happen, but they rarely happen with literary books, which is my bailiwick.

There was a caveat—this agent won't take on clients unless they have at least 50K followers on Instagram. Shocking again.

I've known a number of books now that have come out of New York authored by folks who were adequate writers but who had very hefty followings on social media. Rachel Rodgers's *We Should All Be Millionaires* is one of these (147K followers today), as is Asia Suler's *Mirrors in the Earth* (102K followers today.)

Advance #3

Within the last few months I fielded a much-welcomed offer for
a nonfiction book. The offer was an advance of $4,000. You can
see the terms below. This may be the best that this press can do,
and I hear that. Tectonic plates are shifting in the publishing
biz.

Hardcover: 12.5% to 2,500 copies, 15% for 2,501+ copies sold
Paperback: 10% to 2,500 copies, 12.5% for 2,501+ copies sold
Ebook: 25% to 1,500 copies, 35% for 1,501+ copies
Audiobook: 25% to 1,500 copies, 35% for 1,501+ copies

Royalty advance: $4,000 payable $2,000 on signing and $2,000 on manuscript delivery

That is a "deal" I could not accept.

Advance #4

Also within the last couple of weeks I received a heartwarming
inquiry. A lovely acquisitions editor at a press had read an essay
of mine that published in *The Bitter Southerner* and asked if I
was interested in writing a book about this subject.

"Hearing from you makes me proud," I wrote back.
"Thank you for your interest in a book. Having a phone
conversation about this might be our easiest route forward." I
suggested the phone because I didn't want to write out my
thoughts.

Turns out we couldn't mesh our schedules for a conversation, and I decided not to string the editor along. So I wrote an
email:

> First of all, I thank you again for thinking of me and for being
> in touch. I think it would be the bomb to write a small book
> about this subject; and you seeing the essay in *TBS* and getting
> in contact is a huge honor to me.
>
> I'm in a new place with writing, and I doubt that we can
> work together, so there's no need for a phone conversation

looming on our calendars if there's little chance of this working.

Here's why.

I've always published with small, literary, mission-driven or academic presses. About a year ago I had an epiphany about being a poor, broke artist, and I made the decision that I was done with that life.

This is why I self-published my last book, a novel.

My royalties for my first book were 7.5 and 6.5 percent (from Milkweed Editions, 1999). That royalty rate, combined with a working-class childhood, a poor money mindset, and the fact that I am a woman, kept me in poverty for years. I am no longer in the business of writing to keep middle-people, so to speak, in business. That means publishers, agents, publicists, Amazon, on and on. For years, literally, I had no health insurance, while I worked for folks in the publishing industry who had great salaries, benefits, health insurance, vacations, etc.

I have all that now, and I would never go backward.

Therefore, if you can negotiate a royalty rate of at least 40 percent, I would be glad/delighted/honored to talk with you about a manuscript.

You can see that there's probably no need for us to talk. I'm sure you can find another great writer to do a book on this subject. In fact, I could probably recommend one of my writing students to you.

Thank you again for being in touch. I hope our paths cross one fine day.

Rereading that email now, I do feel a little cringe, that I was audacious enough to write that. That my writing student had just received an offer of a 7% royalty—and was going to accept it because at least it was an offer (!)—probably led to my sauciness. Or is it that I am addicted to honesty?

I received a nice reply. "If any of your former students working on nonfiction reach out for advice about publishers, I hope you'll consider mentioning our press to them. Just, of course, if it comes up organically and they are at a career stage where working with a small publisher might make sense."

I will. Definitely.

None of this is personal. Our society has no malevolence toward writers. The wonderful folks who are buying books would no doubt love to offer decent money. So I have only love for anyone in the publishing industry these days. We are all suffering from late-stage capitalism in a failing market.

Where does this leave us?

Still writing. Hoping for better times. Figuring out other ways to make money.

Where does this leave writers who always have dreamed of publishing a book?

Same. Still writing.

We write because we love to do it and love is free *or* we figure out a way to monetize it that makes sense to us and that doesn't destroy us, our families, our earth, and everything else we love.

Advance #5

To leave you on a hopeful, positive note, a promising young writer friend got a book deal just over a year ago that was a $60K advance for a first book. It's not a cookbook or a Stephen King thriller, and that's a figure I can get behind.

Market your work

My father could sell anything. All my life he ran a junkyard in southern Georgia and his dealings supported him and his family for over 60 years. I, for one, couldn't sell underwear to a naked person. I could give it away—I'm good at that. But my father was an old-time salesman, an entrepreneur. He never lost his belief in the inherent utility and beauty of money. He liked how money made his wallet fat. He liked how it made him feel. He liked what it could do.

He sold tires, carburetors, starters, alternators, axles, transmissions, mufflers, motors, iron and steel, car bodies, and anything with an engine. He sold anything without an engine too.

I remember when he got in the business of Vidalia onions, after these delicacies began to bring attention to south Georgia. My dad bought onions wholesale, bagged them, and traveled town to town in his ragged Mazda pickup, peddling the sweetest onion in the world. He stopped at insurance companies, town halls, courthouses, and banks, places where he'd find working people. He stopped at garages, road departments, and hardware stores.

Daughter

Then in 1999, as an unknown, rank, young, female Southern writer I published a book in which my father appeared as a main character.

The book was due out in early October of that year. A copy, said the publisher, would ship directly from the printer to my door, when for the first time I would hold my own finished book in my hands. After that I could buy copies at an author's discount of 40 percent.

Forty percent was also the bookseller's discount. Our town was without a bookstore. The nearest was in Brunswick, 70 miles east. And October was six months away.

Armed with a Milkweed Editions catalog, my father headed

to town. He visited the mayor, clerk of court, presidents of the
three banks, librarians, bank tellers, secretaries, and cashiers.
Most of these people he knew from a lifetime spent in one
place. Many were people for whom spending 20 bucks on a
book was not insignificant, the average income for Baxley being
about $24,000 at the time.

"My daughter has a book coming out," my dad would say,
"and I thought you might be interested in it."

Or, "Mr. James Kilgo has read the book. He's a professor up
in Athens. He called the book a 'treasure' of knowledge."

"You don't have to pay now," he told his customers. "Wait
until the books arrive."

In this prime market my father pre-sold 200 books. (This
wasn't a self-published book, but I think this is a good time to
say that 90 percent of self-published books sell fewer than 100
copies.)

First printing

When October arrived, the book tour's first stop was my
hometown. Books arrived mere days before the reading. My
father began to deliver them. As people buried themselves in
the story, news shot through town. Daddy's phone began to
ring: "I want a copy of that book your daughter wrote." Or two
copies.

Seventy people showed up at the public library the night of
the book launch. My father set up a table at the back of the
room, where books sold like wildfire. After I spoke, I got busy
signing. I signed for a couple of hours, adding names and dates,
and writing inscriptions as poetic and heartfelt and sincere as I
could. My dad sold another couple hundred.

The volume was hardback and sold for $19.95. I had signed
a royalty contract with Milkweed for 7.5 percent, or 6.5 percent
for copies sold at a discount above 50 percent. This meant that

for every book sold, I made about $1.50 and my father, using the 40% author's discount, grossed $7.98.

From that tidy sum, of course, he had to pay shipping costs and buy diesel for his Mazda pickup, but I thought a lot about those figures. Although I'd completed the first draft during one summer, the book had taken three years to revise and publish, and now my profit was one-fifth of my dad's or of any bookseller's.

My dad kept selling books, ordering them by the box, traveling with and without me. He was loving this. I was surprised at how strategic he was.

Meanwhile, a reporter from *The New York Times* called. She wanted to do a story. She landed at the airport in Savannah, traveling with a photographer, and I met them at a longleaf pine forest on Fort Stewart Military Base, so I could stand knee-deep in wiregrass and be photographed. I was thrilled with the reporter, Anne Raver, who was beautiful and loved gardens and was intrigued with everything about my life, even the hard stuff. She possessed none of the curtness and disdain that I had imagined a New York reporter to have. She saw the forest. She saw the farm where I lived, with its falling-down buildings and arrowheads secreted in a tin in the garden shed. She saw the junkyard where my parents lived, and she meandered through stacked, wrecked, abandoned cars ever sinking into layers of pine needles, my father as her tour-guide.

"How did you come to write?" she asked me, and I told how my father categorized poets with saints, and how I wanted to be counted among them. That story became a full page in *The New York Times,* solid gold.

Second printing

The excitement of being published was a tidal wave. The first print-run of 4,500 sold out, and the book went into a second printing. Then it entered a third. More reporters called, from Tallahassee, Jacksonville, Atlanta, Raleigh, and Chattanooga. Each trip to a wobbly mailbox out by my dirt road brought handfuls of mail, letters from readers, from professors, and from organizers inviting me to exotic places I'd never been.

One day a white van bearing an Illinois license tag pulled into the farmyard. The stranger said he'd read the book, and a map app had provided directions to my door.

Nine months after the book was released, while I was strolling with old friends at a folk festival, someone recognized me from a jacket photograph. The festival was crowded, and people, smiling and nodding, were greeting each other as they passed. This was different. A young man looked pointedly at me as he passed, then turned and caught up. "I read your book," he said.

The marketing was working, be it my fathers or Milkweed's or my own.

More reviews and articles came out. The book won an award, then another. I traveled to libraries and universities and festivals and conferences. I came to believe that story was as powerful as I'd thought it; that Kittredge was correct when he said that people were hungry for truth; and that the way to the heart of my region, the South, was through books. Southerners especially loved a good book, and they treated their authors (I was no exception) like gods.

On hype

Something not so exciting and more problematic was happening too, and I tell you this so that perhaps you can be more prepared than I. Even though the hoopla of being a published book writer was nothing like real fame, being one wrecked my privacy. The phone was ringing, constantly it seemed. Sometimes friendships lost a familiar, ambivalent knowingness that was replaced with something more tense, fraught, and excitable.

I wanted readers. I wanted to make a difference. However, there was a problem.

In becoming an author I destroyed sanctuary. I had annihilated a certain and comforting anonymity. Slowly the solitude and silence from which my work emerged began to be lost. A writer must get up every morning and go alone into the bowels of imagination. When the noon bell rang, I wanted to leave behind those awful mines and be an ordinary person, one who makes soup and plants kale and schedules checkups and plans birthdays and checks out ordinary books from ordinary libraries. Gone were the days I was browser, a calm sheep in wild grasses, ambling through sunlight.

So many thoughts on privacy and anonymity could be expressed here, but all I will do is call to mind James Baldwin's explanation of why he moved to the south of France. "I'm not really, in America, a private person. I'm a public person. A public person cannot write." I can also mention Cormac McCarthy's insistence of living life on his private terms. The problem of being a public person is a condition some of us truly want; some of us want it until it really belongs to us; and some of us never want it. Consider that.

For years afterward I struggled with the tension that sometimes comes when you launch your art into the world, a grinding point of contact between wanting success and not wanting success. If this happens to you, you will have to navigate this carefully. Maybe you will enjoy being a public person more than Baldwin.

Becoming visible

In order to earn the wonderful problem of becoming known, you have to create a great product first and then you have to market. Books don't sell themselves. The author makes the book and puts herself at the mercy of the sellers, but what really sells books are the author's consorts. Word of mouth sells books.

This is why my father was important in my career. At the end of the first year of sales for *Ecology*, my father had sold 1,200 copies out of a total of 10,000 printed.

Selling

Years ago someone gave me Og Mandino's classic, *The Greatest Salesman in the World*. A poor camel boy, Hafid, becomes prosperous by using the wisdom found on 10 ancient scrolls.

Because my dad quit school, and because he ran a junkyard, he wasn't likely, I believed, to have a selling strategy.

But how did he sell so many books? Like hotcakes. How did he sell everything so well?

I called him up. "Daddy. Do you have a philosophy of selling?"

"Of course."

"Would you lay it out for me?"

"Be glad to."

We arranged an interview. That was the day my dad outlined his seven beautiful principles of book-selling. I am charting it here for you.

The product

First, believe in your product. For him, the product was not simply a *book*. My father would not have wasted a minute trying to vend *Gone with the Wind* or *Light in August*, or even *Ecology of a Cracker Childhood*. What Franklin was selling was something anybody could buy—the dream of a son or daughter doing good. If this could happen to Frank Ray, out at the junkyard, it could happen to anybody. In our town he'd always been an underdog, a poor boy, part of the Ray clan with its mental illness, the one sent off, a junk man. He was selling that pride. He was selling a bigger glory, too, that a backwater place had spawned a book.

The demand

Second, create a market. Create interest. Create curiosity. Create a sense of belonging.

Gossip had raced through town. Townspeople heard they were in the book, and they wanted to check how they'd been represented. They wanted some things explained.

Franklin was selling membership to a club, composed of people who knew firsthand what was between the covers. One gentleman purchased a book for himself but his wife absconded with it. She would read the book in the evening, and when she left for work she'd take it with her. The man was dying to read it and couldn't get it away from his wife. His solution was to buy another copy. He wanted to be in the club.

Daddy delivered a copy of the book to one man, Dewayne Yeomans, late in the afternoon at his place of business. Mr. Yeomans was single at the time, and instead of going home, he sat at his desk after closing time and began to read. He didn't stop, he told me later, until he'd read the entire book, finally quitting his office in the wee hours of the morning.

Another man told my father that mine was the *first* book he had read, start to finish.

For a salesman, these are hugely valuable stories. They

create excitement, which is a market. My father used these stories to sell even more books.

Then, like a bird dog seeking coveys of quail, my father had roamed beyond my hometown, going farther afield to peddle. The trunk of his car was jammed with boxes. Now when he peddled he took with him articles from newspapers, including *The New York Times*, laminated.

If an event was close enough for my parents to attend, and return home before 10 or 11 at night, I arranged for them to sell books. Often a few days before a reading my father would canvas a town, carrying with him a flyer I'd made, to drum up interest. He'd visit first the people he might know in the area, visit the venue where the reading was to be held, then visit whomever he found. He was on a mission to tell the world about this book.

The merch

Franklin's third principle was to create supporting products. One afternoon I arrived to my parent's home, planning to drive with them to a reading in Waycross, about an hour away. My mother was wearing a T-shirt with the cover of the book silkscreened on it. Above the cover was my name, and below, the words AUTHOR, ENVIRONMENTALIST, POET. T-shirts were $12.

On a drive to Darien to a book festival, my parents talked about getting a similar design printed on a magnetic panel for the vehicle. I thought by then the marketing had gone too far.

The silver bullet

My father's fourth principle of selling is the most important. Any book sold could turn into a "silver bullet," striking the heart of someone unusually important to a book's success. That someone might be Oprah, or an editor of *The New York Times Review of Books*, or Reese Witherspoon, or a judge for a writers' award. So you treat every customer as if she is Oprah. No matter how poorly dressed, no matter how slow-talking, no matter how shy—a person might, unbeknownst, open a door. Somebody from Podunk might have an aunt who lives next door to somebody who works at the *The New Yorker* or who teaches at Harvard or who's reading for the National Book Awards.

Or somebody might be that someone herself.

This principle harkens to the Biblical admonition, *Be not forgetful to entertain strangers: for thereby some have entertained angels unawares.*

So don't be ungracious, unkind, dismissive, assumptive, or ungrateful in your interactions with folks.

There isn't one silver bullet. There are many. You never know which book might suddenly morph into a silver bullet. So you have to treat each and every book as if might strike the heart of someone who opens a big door. A very big door. A wide and tall door. And treat every potential customer as if they are an angel.

The experience

Fifth, remember that a purchase is not a material item only. A purchase is an experience. A purchaser had the chance to interact with my very interesting father. A purchaser had the chance to connect with the author, since my father had a direct line to me. Any time of day the phone might ring and my father might want me to drop everything and drive the seven miles from my grandmother's farmhouse, where I lived, to the junk-yard. He had somebody who wanted to meet me or who

needed a book signed. Other times, he brought visitors unan-
nounced to my house. A box of books did not arrive without me
signing it immediately. To him, my signature was gold. He
couldn't afford me getting in a car accident with a box of books
unsigned.

The guarantee

Offer a money-back guarantee. If anybody, for any reason, did
not like the book, Franklin would accept it back and fully
refund the person's money. He always offered this. I don't think
it ever happened.

The people

Franklin's last principle of book-selling was: like flies on sticky
paper, nobody escapes. If people stopped at the junkyard to
look for a Hudson side mirror or inquire after a Spartan Impe-
rial Mansion blocking the side yard, they didn't leave until they
had bought a copy of the book. They got the sales pitch for the
book before they could see the Packard.

Once a man stopped at the junkyard to examine a vintage
Studebaker. Of course he left with a copy of *Ecology*, a book sale
propped up by tales and news articles, T-shirts and car signs, a
money-back guarantee. A week later, the man returned. He was
the owner of a chain of breakfast restaurants and was opening
one in town. He wanted to buy 25 copies of the book to
distribute among his board of directors.

Many writers do the routine of loading their car-trunks
with books before traveling to readings. I never wanted to do
that. "I'm not a retailer," I'd say. I was taken up with words, with
saying what I thought people needed to hear to change their
world. Handling money if not diluted then adulterated this

message, I'd say then. But my parents had never made much more than $1,000 a month, and during most of their lives had subsisted on much less. For my books to provide them a supplemental income made me happy.

During the first year that *Ecology of a Cracker Childhood* was out, 1999, three print-runs of hardbounds totaled 10,000 copies. My father sold 1,200 of these—12 percent of the total. He was ordering them straight from the publisher, getting the indie bookstore (and author) discount (40%) and later getting the Amazon discount (50%). One day he and I sat down and added up all the invoices. That's how I know how many he sold.

Meanwhile, the publisher had a beautiful but not unusual strategy for publicizing the book: a collection of blurbs, review copies to book editors and reviewers, direct contact with someone at *The New York Times Review of Books*, a book tour of big Southern cities with well-known independent bookstores, and repeated calls to publicity contacts in those cities.

Of course, yes, the successes of a book can be attributed to a good publicist at a great publishing company. But I don't think that my first book had a better publicist than my dad. Without my dad it might have sunk like a rock.

When the book went into paperback in 2000, my father continued to sell. Now over 200,000 copies of the book have sold (traditional publishers won't tell you exactly how many), the book has won awards, I continue to be invited to read, and campuses still select the book for classes and first-year reading programs. No small part of this success is attributed to my father, the greatest salesman in the world to me.

I, as well, took marketing seriously. I wrote a marketing plan. Times have changed, and this one is slanted toward a rural demographic and occurred before social media took over.

A marketing plan

1. Send a press release by email to all weekly newspapers in your region, attaching a jpg of the cover and an author photo. This is not an ad and needn't cost money.
2. Give readings, anywhere invited. Do it for free, if need be. Later you can charge.
3. Help organizers with publicity. Make a flyer if they don't make one, and send it to them. To this day I create Facebook events and design graphics for organizers. An overworked or timid organizer will not fill a room. Help them. Research a local calendar in their newspaper and send an announcement. If people don't know that you're in town, they don't have a chance to come see you.
4. Create a mailing list. For years I've kept business cards and scribbled numbers on napkins. Finally I hired a student to create a mailing list in an Excel spreadsheet. With a book out, the mailing list was priceless. When I was invited to do a reading, in Charlottesville let's say, I would scramble the mailing list to batch addresses of people within an hour's drive of Charlottesville. I would mail these people hand-written cards, inviting them to the reading, a time-consuming but very effective strategy. To this day I keep curating the list, adding addresses from fan mail and off checks and from business cards.
5. Say *yes* to any interview, even with a student. Invite reporters into your home.
6. Do radio. Some of my favorite publicity has been hundreds of radio and podcast interviews.

None of this—none—is going to do you any good at all unless you can write a good and useful story. So get on with it.

Exercise

Create two mantras, one about writing and one about money, or one mantra with two parts. Write them down and tack them above your mirror or writing desk. Repeat them daily.

Prompt

What holds me back...

28

TESTAMENT

I believe that each of us is born with a mission. Each of us has been given a purpose, and I think that service is always part of our mission. The challenge is to find our purposes and to apprentice ourselves to them.

My purpose has been to use stories to protect the biota of the earth and the ecology of this planet that is our home. Knowing the earth is to return to the essence of who we are, that first we are biological. Culture can be fun and entertaining but before we kept records, before we made laws, before we wrote stories down, we operated out of our bodies as much as our minds, interacting with the wild world. We were embodied. My purpose is to remain in that wild body, honor what it is, and protect what it needs.

My purpose is to midwife the survival of the human species.

My purpose is to speak for the planet as well as for species who have no agency, authority, or voice.

A whole and functional planet means that human community gets a better chance to be whole and functional. It means that we individually get a better chance to be whole and functional.

My purpose is to rebuild communities, human and wild, because in community we find resilience.

Reasons to hide

The pandemic caused a lot of damage to human community. It caused us to distrust, shun, and hide our faces from each other. What we really distrusted was a virus, but the virus got confused with people. We became more fearful.

The devolution of democracy causes some folks to shun politics.

Now the climate chaos is upon us—we know the climate emergency can enter our own homes at any time, and that causes us to think about survival.

Threat can make us close off, lay low, be careful. Threat can keep us from doing the lovely things that have been part and parcel of a good life, like having parties, joining softball leagues, volunteering. Going to book readings, attending book club meetings. Dressing up and going out to cultural events.

Threat, of course, is not the only reason humans are more isolated than ever. There's technology always jitterbugging around to steal our attention away from community.

Given the pandemic, politics, climate chaos, and the weirdness of digital life it's easy to want to stay small.

I ask you

I am going to ask a huge favor. In any way that you have begun to close off, give up, not care, lay low, and isolate yourself—I ask you to rethink this. This is not the time to stay small. This is the time to get big.

You're a writer. Writing is hard. Your work gets rejected a lot. You get passed over for awards and grants. You go underpaid or unpaid.

I'm asking you to keep telling the stories you've been given.

Once I heard a chaplain pray at a commencement at Warren Wilson College, a college in the mountains of western North Carolina that asks its students to *Think deeply. Care fiercely. Work hard.* This chaplain said that there's a lot of work to be done. Much of it is to be done in far corners of the world, with little fanfare or acknowledgement, and with limited resources. He offered a new crop of graduates to god.

"Put them in hard places," he said.

Much of the work of art is to be done in far corners, daily, invisibly, with little succor and with limited resources.

But...

Only by telling stories—connecting people, offering epiphanies, imagining new and just narratives, replacing destructive narratives—can we create a world that helps us lead more meaningful, sensible, functional, and fulfilling lives.

The violence in Israel and the Gaza Strip is gutwrenching. I imagine people trying to lead sensible, functional, fulfilling lives with rockets flying, limited food, and no electricity. The narrative in the Middle East, to offer one example, is an old, useless narrative. It is beyond time for a new narrative.

I cast my lot with those who—with few extraordinary powers, with hearts full of love—continue the work required to reconstitute and heal ourselves, our relationships, and this wild, beloved, broken, beleaguered world.

In closing

Remember, the stories are not going to get told unless you do your part. And we're not going to change what needs to be changed unless we abandon our silences. Yes, it's hard work, but you know how to work hard. Being a good writer may not happen fast, but incrementally, piece by piece, you can claim your voice, refine your craft, immerse yourself in magic's current, and build a body of important work.

All this to say, *Do the hard work. Do it bigger than ever.*

Who needs your stories? You do. We all do.

May your stories be easy to find and to write.

~

Exercise

Write a flash essay about one of your heroes, especially if you've been able to meet them.

~

Prompt

I believe...

~

THE END

1

APPENDIX: HOW TO REWILD

Here's a list of ideas, in no particular order, for rewilding. Many of these came from brainstorms with other writers during writing workshops.

I PURPOSEFULLY STRAND myself in a cabin with no running water or electricity.

I swim in a river, especially when I first arrive to a place.

I spend lots of time walking and running, exploring back alleys and far trails.

I expose myself to the elements.

I get lost.

I'm quiet.

I garden.

I watch birds.

I do something physically strenuous.

I eat organically.

I forage and wildcraft.

I hunt.

I try something I didn't think I could do.

I walk barefoot.

I meditate.

I try to find something I probably cannot find.

I lie prostrate with my nose and my hands on the earth.

I celebrate earth holidays like solstice.

I dance.

I hike.

I exercise.

I move my body.

I identify trees and plants.

I practice naturism, meaning I stay outside naked.

I swim until I'm tired.

I touch the trees and bushes and flowers as I walk past.

I eat something really delicious.

I sing.

I talk to a stranger.

I turn inward instead of outward.

Or I do the opposite.

I pet a toad.

I ask the earth for guidance.

I identify my primary archetypes and try to embody them.

I sleep in bear country.

I know the tides.

I take risks.

I go outside and look up at the stars.

I learn the names of the constellations, planets, and stars.

I greet the creatures around me.

I whistle back to the birds.

I talk to plants.

I surround myself with natural textiles.

I eat seasonally.

I shop at the farmers market.

I cook using whole foods.

I disconnect from the digital world.

I build fires and cook over them.

I rely on plants for medicine and guidance.

I drink mugwort tea before bed.

I make ancient herbal beers.

I do psychedelics.

I ground, my bare feet and sometimes my entire body against the ground.

I wear leather-soled shoes.

I make notes of phenology—when flowers are blooming, birds are migrating, and so forth.

I read field guides.

I keep a phenology notebook.

I sleep on the ground.

I sit under a tree.

I climb trees.

I identify wildflowers and trees.

I study animal tracks.

I take field notes on animal behavior.

I have sex outdoors.

I learn birdsong.

I collect things from nature without doing harm—dropped feathers or small stones.

~

Exercise

Do some of these things.

~

Prompt

I am wildest when...

2

APPENDIX: WHY WRITE ABOUT NATURE

To document, so that others may know what you saw and knew and thought.
To interpret science.
To introduce new ideas.
To show loss.
To offer hope.
To make change.
To let future generations know you did all you could to protect our common ecological heritage.
To be voices of the land, like a Lorax speaking for the trees.
"To evoke, honestly, some single aspect of all that the land contains" (Barry Lopez, from *Crossing Open Ground*).
To capture nature before it's lost.
To provide access to wild places.
To soothe souls.
To write about ourselves since we *are* nature.
To get back in touch with tangibles.
To learn ancient knowledge.
To witness nature's violence and to accept that violence.
To explore the intelligences of nonhumans.

To learn from the land.
To reinvent the world.
To record culture.
To show the damage we're doing to the earth.
To protest.
To connect the dots.
To mourn.
To grieve the destruction of what we love.
To call for a moment of silence.
To get intimate with the natural world.
To create that intimacy for others.
To put a place on the map.

Exercise

Visit a library and find the shelves on nature. See what's there.

Prompt

I write about nature because...

3

APPENDIX: GIVE A GREAT READING

W hen a writer stands up to give a reading, a current of energy whips around the room.

The energy is heightened expectation. The better-known the writer, the higher the energy. Sitting in an audience, a person wonders—is this person going to turn my world upside down? Will this be an hour I never forget?

Or will this be an hour spent trapped in an outer ring of hell?

I've been a book-writer since 1999, and in those two decades I've given *hundreds* of talks. I've felt that current, over and over and over, enough to know that it is not an electricity to be ignored. I'm probably more scared of it now than I was when I gave my first reading. I'm also not saying that I give great readings, only that I've learned a few things about the stage, and I want to share these with you, so that when your next turn comes to get up and throw lightning bolts around a room, you'll be better prepared.

What you should know

You feel like a hero standing up in front of folks, but you're not the hero. The audience members are the heroes. If they were absent, you wouldn't have a reading. You'd be calling for an Uber so you could go back to the Econolodge. Having an audience is a gift. Don't take it for granted.

An audience understands the energy of a speaker very quickly and responds accordingly. You only have a few minutes to get on course.

You are not delivering something all tied up in a pretty pink bow. This is not a delivery. It is an interaction. A reading is not about *I*, it's about *we*.

Don't waste anybody's time, not even your own.

Try to create an energy in the room that keeps would-be sleepers awake and wakes the sleepers. Such an energy cannot be created by becoming louder. It can't be created with thriller drama. It's created by a feeling—a power field—that story creates around itself, that you create with delivery, and that the audience creates with expectation and breathlessness.

More than tense waiting is involved, however.

Try to levitate the room.

Levitate a room

Being nervous is okay—your nervousness adds to the energy—but it's wasted if you talk fast. Make yourself slow down. Enunciate.

You've already had an epiphany because you wrote the pieces you're reading. That's your gift to the audience. So now others are having a transformation. Let them.

Audience members are giving you something in return. They are giving you their

- attention.
- inattention.
- laughter.
- tears.
- sharp intakes of breath.
- slow out-breaths.
- tears rolling down cheeks.

Later they give you their questions.

The benefits

What can be gained from writers reading their works in person?

- Well, the reader can engage with the writer.
- The reader can hear the words as the writer meant them to be heard.
- The writer can make words come alive for the reader.
- The writer can make herself come alive and can become an entity the reader wants to support.
- The reader, now in the writer's community, may want to widen the circle by buying copies of books to give away.

Pointers

Do not judge an audience by the reactions visible to you. I've made that mistake dozens of times. I leave a stage thinking, *How stone-faced. They hated me.* Then in the signing line I hear glowing comments that are big-hearted enough to float a cruise ship.

One dude nodding off can ruin a great performance. Speak

to everybody else, not to him. Hope nobody else is seeing him nap.

If possible, train yourself to speak off-script. I have no judgement if you stand behind a podium and read from a paper—this has taken me years and years, but I'm finally getting there. Not relying on a page is powerful.

Memorize at least some of your work. Entire poems or paragraphs are great (necessary for spoken word) but even sentences or phrases are good. This is super-impressive.

Why not avoid PowerPoints and let the rhythm, lyricism, and magic of language carry you through?

Ninety-five percent of talks begin with obligatory thanks. For years now I have tried to start with something different, to surprise audience members right from the get-go. I stand up and shock listeners by starting with a poem or lyrical paragraph—one I've memorized—that lasts a minute or two. Then I quickly express gratitude and get the train rolling down the track.

Humor here is priceless. I'm too intense to be a funny person—we're trying to save the world here, people—so I force myself to include some one-liners. Normally I'm opposed to self-deprecating humor, but it goes a long way when a writer (some of the most egotistical people in the world) takes the stage.

I employ eye contact. In the early days, I tried to meet every person's eye in the auditorium at least once. This makes some people nervous. You can tell when people get nervous because they quickly look away if your eyes land on them. Make a mental note to look elsewhere. Let your eyes wander. Cover the entire auditorium. I say this because when I'm in an audience, I love the feeling I get when a famous speaker—Jane Goodall, for instance—looks directly at me. I feel seen. So make others feel seen.

Wear clothing that's interesting but not attention-seeking.

Some unforgettable readings

Many years ago I heard Richard Nelson, author of *The Island Within* and other books on Alaska, tell the story of touching a deer on a wild island near Sitka. That scene starts on page 272 in the book, in case you're looking.) When Nelson returned home, as he explained, guests were visiting, but the event had been so powerful that he had to excuse himself to process what had just happened. Onstage reading this passage he recreated the same wild and chance energy, until the auditorium was silent, hundreds of people leaning forward, tense, breaths bated, waiting to hear what happened.

I always love hearing Pattiann Rogers read her poetry. That is a jewel of an hour. I loved hearing Mary Oliver read at a church in Provincetown—I hung on to every word.

Once I was on a Forgotten Language Tour with *Orion* Magazine in the Yaak Valley of Montana. A freak storm hit that day. The writers were out in woods, looking around, when trees began to whip about and crash to the ground. The storm, some kind of microburst, was terrifying. That night a few writers were to read in a local lodge. Although the electricity was out, the reading went on by candlelight. Rick Bass read "Swamp Boy," a piece of autofiction about a bullied child who loves nature. That was one of the most poignant readings I've ever heard. I wept through most of it.

In each of these cases the writer used energy to levitate a room. You can too. When your turn comes to read, don't give a boring reading, because I hate drooling in public.

4

APPENDIX: MAPS AND SCROLLS

Ackerman, Diane. *The Moon by Whale Light.*

Bass, Rick. Nonfiction, particularly *The Book of Yaak*. Also the essay "Hold Nothing Back," among many others.

Basso, Keith. *Wisdom Sits in Places.*

Beard, Jo Ann. "The Fourth State of Matter," *The New Yorker*, June 24 and July 1, 1996. This is a perfect essay.

Berry, Wendell. Anything, especially *In the Presence of Fear* and *Collected Poems.*

Blunt, Judy. *Breaking Clean*, the opening essay in the book of the same name.

Brown, Larry. *Joe,* among others.

Buhner, Stephen Harrod. *Ensouling Language*. Order it now. And try out everything else he has written. (Sometimes he repeats himself.)

Cather, Willa. Anything, certainly *My Antonia.*

Cerulean, Susan. *Tracking Desire*. Plus.

Corrie, Daniel. His poetry about time and longleaf pines.

Faulkner, William. Anything and all.

Fisher-Wirth, Ann. Fabulous poetry. *Blue Windows* is my favorite.

Frazier, Charles. *Cold Mountain*, of course.

Galvin, James. *The Meadow.*

Gay, William. Any of the novels published during his lifetime.

Godin, Seth. *The Practice: Shipping Creative Work* and *This is Marketing: You Can't Be Seen Until You Learn to See.*

Gruchow, Paul. *Grassroots: The Universe of Home.*

Haworth, Holly. Essays, especially "A Return to Feeling" in the anthology *Solastalgia,* edited by Paul Bogard.

Haruf, Kent. All those amazing novels.

Hurston, Zora Neale. *Their Eyes Were Watching God.*

Kilgo, James. *Deep Enough for Ivorybills* is fine old-school southern nature writing.

King, Jr., Dr. Martin Luther. Golden speeches.

Kingsolver, Barbara. *Poisonwood Bible. Small Wonder.*

Kittredge, William. *Taking Care: Thoughts on Storytelling and Belief.*

Lakoff, George. *Don't Think of an Elephant.*

Lopez, Barry. *Home Ground: A Literary Guide to Landscape Terms.*

Mahood, Kim. "Listening is harder than you think," *The Griffith Review* #19.

Marquez, Gabriel Garcia. Yes.

McCarthy, Cormac. Especially *All the Pretty Horses* and *Cities of the Plain* (a masterpiece).

McKibben, Bill. *Hope, Human and Wild.* Plus.

McLean, Sorley. Poetry.

McPhee, John. If you want to write about nature, read McPhee. You'll need years to read everything. His book on craft, *Draft No. 4,* I highly recommend. Also *Encounters with the Archdruid.*

Merwin, W.S. Do not skip his poetry.

Moore, Kathleen Dean. Read Derrick Jensen's interview with her in *The Sun*, March 2001, "A Weakened World Cannot Forgive Us."

Nabhan, Gary.

Neruda, Pablo. Start with *Selected Poems*.

O'Connor, Flannery. All of *Mystery and Manners*, especially the chapter "Writing Short Stories" and "The Regional Writer."

Oliver, Mary. Her poetry. She should have been poet laureate of the globe. *Upstream* is a great book of essays.

Orion Magazine. Nature writing. Especially old issues.

Penn, Joanna. *The Creative Penn Podcast* as well as wonderful books on current trends in indie publishing.

Petterson, Per. *Out Stealing Horses*. Great Norwegian writer. Great.

Rawlings, Marjorie Kinnan. *The Yearling* and *Cross Creek*. If she fascinates you, read Ann McCutchan's fine biography, *The Life She Wished to Live*.

Ray, Janisse. (That's me.) Read everything! And get your library to buy my books! Especially *Ecology of a Cracker Childhood* and *Wild Spectacle* and *The Seed Underground* and *The Woods of Fannin County*.

Rich, Adrienne. "Women and Honor: Some Notes on Lying," from the book *On Lies, Secrets, and Silence*.

Roy, Arundhati. Essays. Every one.

Sanders, Scott Russell. "Writing from the Center," essay published in *The Georgia Review*.

Shepherd, Nan. *The Living Mountain* (Scottish nature writer). Oh my god.

Silko, Leslie Marmon. *Ceremony*.

Snyder, Don. "Winter Work," essay.

Sojourner, Mary. "Belly," essay from *Sierra* Magazine.

Terrain.org. Some great nature writing these days is coming from *Terrain*.

Villasenor, Daniel. *The Lake*.

Wainwright, Alfred. *A Pennine Journey: The Story of a Long Walk in 1938.*

Walker, Alice. *The Color Purple.*

Williams, Terry Tempest. *Refuge.*

Wilson, E.O. *Biophilia.*

Zinn, Howard. *Artists in Times of War.*

GRATITUDE

Thank you, reading this, for giving this book a chance. For all my books you've read. For purchasing and checking out and recommending and donating and passing on to others. For being my friend in life and on social media. Thank you. Also for your love of books and stories, for your hope for the planet, for your labors in stabilizing communities around you. I'm grateful to all who understand that we're all part of something bigger than ourselves, that we are tasked with the stewardship of creation, and that we are responsible for each other and all living things.

Teachers

Over the years of my writing life, many teachers have helped me, and I thank them: Wendell Berry, Sharon Blackie, Steve Bodio, Stephen Harrod Buhner, Jerry Carter, Lucille Clifton, Elsa Gaines, Jack Gilbert, Seth Godin, Hank Harrington, Amber Magnolia Hill, Annie Ruth Howard, William Kittredge, Coach John O'Brien, Joanna Penn, Steven Pressfield, David

Raby, Rachel Rodgers, Annick Smith, Patricia Traxler, Alan Weisman, and Sonia Williams.

Editors & Agents

I've worked with fine editors over the years, including Chip Blake, Emilie Buchwald, Stephen Corey, Daniel Corrie, Brianne Goodspeed, Larry Kopczak, Eric NeSmith, Chuck Reece, Jennifer Sahn, Paul Sutter, and Jan Winburn. I thank you. Thanks to my agents past and present, Madison Smartt Bell, Philippa Brophy, Jeff Dwyer, Leigh Feldman, Elizabeth Grossman, and Sam Stoloff.

Colleagues

Thanks to folks with whom I've worked on various projects: Rick Bass, Megan Mayhew Bergman, Wendell Berry, David Brown, Susan Cerulean, Dorinda Dallmeyer, Jeff Dwyer, Jane Fishman, Peggy Galis, Toby Graham, Linda Hogan, James Holland, John Lane, J. Drew Lanham, Angela Faye Martin, Brent Martin, Peter Matthiessen, Bill McKibben, Kathleen Dean Moore, Dink NeSmith, Paul Pressly, Annick Smith, Betsy Teter, Terry Tempest Williams, James Wohlpart, and many more. Thanks to colleagues at the Hargrett Rare Book and Manuscript Library, University of Georgia.

Hollins University, via the Susan Jackson Writer-in-Residence grant, gave me time to concentrate on this book. I thank Thorpe Moeckel, Holly Haworth, Marilyn Moriarty, Richard Dillard, Cathryn Hankla, Jeanne Larsen, and Susan Jackson for that opportunity. Some of this book took shape after John Lane invited me to do a 20-year retrospective of *Ecology of a Cracker Childhood* at Wofford College in Spartanburg in 2019. For that specifically I thank scholars John Lane, Dorinda Dallmeyer, Tara Powell, and Peter K. Brewitt. Stephen Corey, then editor of

The Georgia Review, published two pieces of this manuscript in the Fall 2019 issue under the title "Now, Looking Back." I thank Stephen, as well as Caroline "C.J." Bartunek and Doug Carlson.

Erin Kirk designed the cover and interior of this book. A painting by Raven Waters is on the cover. The author photograph is by Michelle Holloway. To work with pros like these is a blessing.

Students

Thanks to my students over the years, every one.

Family & Friends

Thanks to my parents, Franklin D. Ray (1937-2019) and Lee Ada Branch Ray, for giving me life. Thanks to my clan: Dr. Thomas and Kay Ray Amsler; Rita Carter; Maureen DeVos; the Mendez family—Joette, Lazaro, Julian, and Nya; Danny and Cherie Montanez Perez; Dell Ray; Carlin J. Ray; and Skye Ray-Waters.

I will always be grateful to Milton N. Hopkins, Jr., a beloved friend who lives on in a starry fold of the universe.

Thanks to Eve Allen, Deb Bowen, Alec Bruns, Susan Cerulean, Kimberly Coburn, Dan Corrie, Ellen Corrie, Steven Croft, Rosemary Daniell, Amanda Dixon, Campbell Dixon, Ann Fisher-Wirth, Sam Ghioto, Holly Haworth, Jeanne Malmgren, Rachel Michaud, Erika Patoni, and Kate Van Cantfort for deepening my writing life. Thanks to many dear friends.

Loving thanks to Sandy Strother Hudson, who made a space in her heart for me and for this book.

Abiding love to Raven Waters and to Silas Ray-Burns.

ABOUT JANISSE RAY

Janisse Ray is an American writer who has been speaking on behalf of nature for over 30 years. Her environmental memoir, *Ecology of a Cracker Childhood*, was a *New York Times* Notable. She has won an American Book Award, Pushcart Prize, Southern Bookseller Award, Southern Environmental Law Center Writing Award, Nautilus Award, and Eisenberg Award, among many others. A recent collection of essays, *Wild Spectacle*, won the Donald L. Jordan Prize for Literary Excellence, which carries a $10,000 prize. Ray earned an MFA from the University of Montana, has received two honorary doctorates, and was inducted into the Georgia Writers Hall of Fame. She lives on an organic farm located inland from Savannah, Georgia. Her passions include dark chocolate, any kind of wildflower, and the blues.

Website | www.janisseray.com
Substack | tracklesswild.substack.com
Email | tracklesswild@gmail.com
Facebook | www.facebook.com/ReadJanisseRay
Instagram | @janisseray_writer
LinkedIn | Janisse Ray

A REQUEST FROM JANISSE

Share

Would you please share this book with friends, family, and neighbors or recommend it to others? Thank you. You may want to ask your librarian to obtain a copy for your local library. Telling friends about meaningful books is still the best way to allow a story to do its job, which is to touch us, open our hearts, and make us think.

In addition, reading a book in tandem with friends or a book club provides common ground for satisfying conversations about questions, ideas, and situations raised in the book. To that end, you may want to suggest this to your book club or writer's group.

I deeply appreciate your assistance in spreading the word to others who may benefit from this book.

Order directly

I hope you will order books directly from me. This can happen via my website. This gives me the opportunity to sign and personalize your books; all you need to do is specify your preferences on your online order. I take great precautions to ensure a secure site, and I attempt to mail books with two business days of receiving the order.

Post

I greatly appreciate your posts on social media, especially those that include a picture of you and the book. Please tag me: @JanisseRay

Possible hashtags you may use in posts include:

#craft&current
#janisseray
#writingcraft
#amwriting
#writingmagic
#magicalcraft
#nonfiction
#story
#newread
#bookinmyhand
#bookclub
#tracklesswild

Review

Unlike most books, this book does not include endorsements from other writers, and instead it relies on the opinions of readers like you. If the book helped you and you have a moment to spare, I would appreciate a review. I'm deeply grateful for articles in your newsletters, blogs, videos, broadcasts, print media, and online journals—as well as stars and notes on Goodreads, Amazon, and other book sites. For a review copy, please be in touch.

Subscribe

To get weekly tips and thoughts on writing, I invite you to sign up for my free newsletter for writers, The Rhizosphere. I'd also love your company at the newsletter that contains my essays and other writing, Trackless Wild, also free.

Socialize

Facebook | www.facebook.com/ReadJanisseRay
Instagram | @janisseray_writer
LinkedIn | Janisse Ray

Contact

To arrange an interview, speaking engagement, workshop, or virtual visit, please contact me via my website, www.janisseray.com.

Your support of books, reading, and writers makes work like this possible. I thank you.

Your friend,

Janisse Ray

Made in the USA
Columbia, SC
30 January 2025

53010658R00186